The Daily T

VAT

A WORKING GUIDE FOR THE SMALL BUSINESS

The Daily Telegraph

VAT

A WORKING GUIDE FOR THE SMALL BUSINESS

Ian Hills

Published by Telegraph Publications
83 Clerkenwell Road, London EC1R 5AR

© Telegraph Publications/William Curtis Publishing

This book is sold subject to the condition that it shall not, by way of trade or otherwise, be lent, re-sold, hired out or otherwise circulated without the publisher's prior consent in any form of binding or cover other than that in which it is published.

All rights reserved. No part of this work may be reproduced or transmitted by any means without permission.

Whilst every care has been taken to ensure the accuracy of the contents of this work, no responsibility for loss occasioned to any person acting or refraining from action as a result of any statement in it can be accepted.

Typeset by BSC Print Limited

Printed in Great Britain

British Library Cataloguing in Publication Data

Hills, Ian
   Small business guide to tax: VAT
   1. Value-added tax — Great Britain
   I. Title
   336.2'714'0941   HJ5715.G7
   ISBN 0-86367-113-6

The VAT Forms reproduced in this book are Crown copyright and are reproduced with the kind permission of HMSO.

Contents

Chapter			
	1	Introduction to Value Added Tax	7
	2	Different types of VAT and how they affect your business	13
	3	Registration	19
	4	Selecting a scheme for your business	29
	5	Input tax	41
	6	Output tax	47
	7	The VAT invoice	55
	8	VAT returns	61
	9	Particular situations relating to your business	69
	10	VAT planning	79
	11	Dealing with HM Customs and Excise	85
	12	De-registration	91
Appendix	I	Local VAT offices listing	97
	II	VAT trade classification	103
	III	Fixed retail mark-ups	113
	IV	How to check the validity of the VAT Registration Number on invoices received	115
Index			117

1 Introduction to Value Added Tax

As Benjamin Franklin once said, 'In this world nothing can be said to be certain, except death and taxes' and one such tax is Value Added Tax (VAT). Unlike other taxes this one is administered by HM Customs and Excise.

VAT was first introduced in the UK on 1 April 1973 as a replacement for purchase tax and selective employment tax and was part of the process of bringing the UK tax system into line with that of the European Community (EEC). In fact, its general principles are governed by EEC directives whose ultimate objective is to harmonise the operation of the tax throughout all member states. Part of the yield from our VAT collections is used to finance the UK's contribution to the EEC budget.

Subsequent UK Government policy is taking us away from direct taxation (with the abolition of development land tax, investment income surcharge, capital transfer tax, etc.) towards indirect taxation. This affects most transactions entered into not only by businesses, but also by individuals, charities and associations, the latter two of which are not normally subject to tax.

VAT is, in effect, a self-assessing system administered by the businessman who, as a consequence, has frequent direct contact with the officers of HM Customs and Excise. Essentially the burden falls on the final consumer of the goods in a 'cascading system', as illustrated in Table 1. VAT is collected in stages from the primary producers via manufacturers, wholesalers, etc., down the line to all purchasers – you and me, the end-users.

HM Customs and Excise officers have the legal right to examine the records and accounts of registered traders at any time (see Chapter 11). Indeed, their powers are far more stringent that those of the police or the Inland Revenue and the penalties for default far more severe, as you will recall from cases recently brought before the Courts.

VAT – A working guide for the small business

Table 1: Illustration of the working of VAT at 15 per cent

Phase	Tax excl. price £	VAT £	Tax incl. price £	Tax payable to C & E £	Paid by
Supply of raw materials to TV manufacturer	200	30	230	30	Supplier
Sold to manufacturer	300	45	345	15 (£45-£30)	Manufacturer
Wholesale marking up	400	60	460	15 (£60-£45)	Wholesaler
Shop	600	90	690	30 (£90-£60)	Customer
	—	—	—	90	

The legislation governing VAT was recently consolidated into the 1983 Value Added Tax Act (VATA) and further amendments to the present working system are planned for 1988. These latest proposals were brought about because the system was perceived to be so time-consuming for the small businessman. The Conservative Government therefore asked HM Customs and Excise to consider ways of relieving this burden. These suggestions are being considered. As far as small exporting businesses are concerned, the alterations proposed for April 1988 (see Chapter 6) to the current VAT rules will alter them again. It is therefore of the utmost importance that you, the businessman, fully understand the workings of the VAT system.

Since its introduction, the rate of tax has altered from the original 10 per cent through a two-tiered system (8 per cent standard rate and 12.5 per cent for luxury goods), to its current level of 15 per cent on all chargeable goods. This became effective on 18 June, 1979. (Exemptions and zero-rated items are dealt with in the following chapters.) There are currently in excess of 1.4 million VAT registered traders who collect some £18 billion on behalf of the government.

The small businessman must be aware that if at any time he believes his future taxable turnover will exceed £21,300 (an increase effective from 17 March 1987 on the previous threshold of £20,500) he *must* register for VAT. This is done by filling in Form VAT1 and sending it to the Customs and Excise immediately. The quarterly turnover threshold has also been increased from £7,000 to £7,250 from the same date. Although you must notify the Customs and Excise if your turnover exceeds that figure in any one quarter, you do not need to be registered if the turnover for the following three quarters falls below the limit, providing you can satisfy the Customs and Excise that this is in fact the case. This is of particular importance to seasonal traders, where the majority of income is earned within a limited period. Chapter 3 gives more comprehensive information.

This book is intended as a step-by-step guide to help small businesses unravel the seemingly complex subject of VAT and to show them that VAT need not be considered a frightening and mysterious tax. By reading and digesting the information contained in the following chapters, the businessman should be able to set up an easy, self-administered system which will ease his workload and alleviate the potential danger to his business that can be caused by neglecting the VAT regulations.

VAT-A working guide for the small business is up-to-date as of May 1987. However, changes are continuously being made and readers are recommended to check with HM Customs and Excise on any new rulings not covered in this book.

VAT terms and common usage

During the course of the book reference will be made to certain terminology used by HM Customs and Excise. It is important for you to become familiar with them and they are defined below. However, should further clarification be needed, contact your local Customs and Excise Office. A list of addresses can be found in Appendix I at the back of this book.

Business: For VAT purposes, the word 'business' has an extremely wide meaning. It can include not only any venture considered to be a trade but also any **trade** (i.e. plumbers, shopkeepers, garages, etc.), **profession** (i.e. solicitors, accountants, etc.) or **vocation** (i.e. any interest, including hobbies, from which money is gained. This would include piano teachers, artists and others who sell their work or services for financial gain.) In addition, the definition of a business could, for example, include a sports club, parent teachers' association or charitable organisation where a subscription is rendered in exchange for the use of facilities.

Furthermore, any activity which is likely to continue and which involves the making or the supply of any goods or the provision of services is chargeable, even if those supplies are made on an irregular basis or on a non-profit making basis.

Exempt supply: Certain types of goods and services are exempted from VAT by law (see Chapter 2). A business which makes just such an exempt supply cannot charge VAT to its customers unless, in addition, it also makes taxable supplies. In such cases this type of business is not required to register for VAT purposes. These exempt supplies include certain transactions in land and financial services and should be segregated from items which are completely outside the scope of VAT in this country, e.g. the payment of salaries, stamp duty and the supply of services outside the UK.

VAT – A working guide for the small business

A person who is registered for VAT cannot, under any circumstances, reclaim from Customs and Excise the value of any VAT charged on his purchase of goods or services which are attributable to an exempt supply.

Goods: Surprisingly, the Value Added Tax Act does not specifically define goods. However, the supply of goods can, for all intents and purposes, be regarded as including all tangible items of a moveable nature. In addition, interests in property (land, houses or business premises) under the law on the supply of goods has been stated to include the following five points:

(1) The transfer of the whole of that property or possession of the 'goods' under a sale agreement on payment in full of that item.

(2) The creation of goods by the application of a process to that item that belongs in law to another person.

(3) The supply in any form of heat, ventilation, refrigeration or power.

(4) The disposal of any business asset for no payment where the cost to that business exceed £10.

(5) The granting, surrender or assignment of a major interest in 'land', as defined above.

Input tax: In effect this is relief allowed for the tax charged on goods and services supplied to the business person in the course of carrying on trading activities. In order to reclaim the tax paid, a number of tests have to be met, namely:

(a) that the tax arose on the supply of goods or services;

(b) in the case of the tax arising on a supply, that supply must have been to the claimant;

(c) that claimant must be a taxable person for VAT purposes at the time of supply;

(d) the VAT must actually be due and payable, thus excluding relief for VAT that has been charged in error;

(e) the tax arose in respect of goods and services which are, or will be, used in the conduct of the claimant's business;

(f) the supply is not one that is designated as disallowable, i.e. business entertainment;

(g) the claim can be supported by documentary evidence, such as a tax invoice.

Even when all the above tests can be satisfied, a partial restriction may well apply in claiming input tax *if* the business is making both exempt and taxable supplies. It is, therefore, essential to recognise this fact well in advance in order to avoid the additional expense to your business.

Output tax: This is the tax you have to charge to your customers on all the taxable supplies that you make (excluding those which are zero rated), provided you are registered for VAT purposes and are, therefore, yourself a taxable person. The current rate of tax is 15 per cent and once collected is paid to HM Customs and Excise, less the amount of input tax you have already suffered.

Positive rate: Currently 15 per cent, this is a rate of VAT other than that known as 'zero rate' and as such is known as the standard rate upon which VAT charges are based.

Registered person: A registered person is one who is normally a taxable person (see below). However, a taxable person can often include someone who should be registered for VAT but for whatever reason has failed to do so. It is most important that readers recognise that it is not their business but they themselves, or group of people carrying on business, that has to be registered for VAT (see Chapter 3). Registration covers all the businesses carried on by the person or group. This can be legally avoided, for example, by the creation of a partnership with somebody else (see Chapter 10 on VAT planning).

Services: The supply of a service is often not so easily identified as the supply of goods. However, legislation dictates that anything which is not a supply of goods but something for which work is done is a 'supply of services'.

Taxable person: A taxable person is considered to be one who makes taxable supplies whilst required to be registered. Please note that the definition of a 'person' includes individuals, companies, partnerships, nationalised bodies, public corporations or even incorporated associations or trustees.

Taxable supplies: As a rule VAT in the UK will apply to the supply of all goods or services within this country by a registered person in the course and conduct of his business. It also applies to the importation of goods from overseas by any person other than in the case of an exempt supply. Supply principally means the supply of goods or services but can also refer to hire purchase transactions, the hiring of equipment or plant and the exchange or granting of a right, for example, over land.

The principle term 'taxable supply' will include both zero and positive rated supplies. Business people should note that any items taken for their own personal use are regarded as a taxable supply. This is where many traders are caught out and extra VAT charges are made against their businesses. As mentioned previously, free gifts or the loan of goods are classed as supplies and may be taxable. However, services that have been rendered without charge are not taxable.

Summarised simply this means that a supply of goods or services made in the UK by a taxable person, other than one which is an exempt supply as previously defined, is liable for VAT.

VAT – A working guide for the small business

Zero rated supply: Not to be confused with an 'exempt supply'. Under UK law, a zero rated supply is, surprisingly, taxable but the tax due is at zero per cent! The goods and services to which zero rating applies are dealt with in the following chapter.

For some exporting businesses, VAT is exempt when goods or services are supplied to member EEC countries.

2 Different types of VAT and how they affect your business

So far we have mentioned briefly the mechanics of VAT and its implementation as a cascade method of taxation, on the assumption that all the inputs and outputs of your business are taxable at a positive rate. It has also been noted that there are certain types of supply your business will be making which command special treatment, either because they are 'zero rated' or because they are 'exempt'. Let us examine these two very different categories in more detail.

The first to be discussed is zero rated VAT. It is useful at this stage to remember that if a supply is zero rated no tax is charged on the supply, but credit is given to the supplier for all tax on his inputs relating to that supply. The export of goods, for instance, falls within this category. (This means that goods can leave this country free of VAT, although they may be liable to have VAT levied on them upon entry into the country of importation.) Thus, a business which deals exclusively with the export of manufactured goods will find that in its accounting period for VAT inputs will exceed outputs, resulting in a repayment from HM Customs and Excise.

Zero rated categories

There are 18 groups which carry a zero rate of VAT, and it is useful to examine these briefly. All have been included, although subsequently amended, since the 1972 Finance Act.

(1) **Food:** Most food for consumption by humans and animals falls within this category. The exceptions are pet food, alcoholic drinks, ice cream, chocolate, potato crisps and soft drinks, as well as any food supplied in the course of catering. Since 1 May 1984 this has also included hot, take-away food and drinks.

(2) **Sewage services and the supply of water:** The exceptions to this group include distilled and bottled water.

VAT – A working guide for the small business

(3) **Books:** Basically all printed material, including all books, newspapers, magazines, sheet music and pamphlets. However, items such as posters, stationery and diaries remain taxable.

(4) **Talking books for the blind and handicapped and radios for the blind:** Zero rating provisions do apply to any equipment adapted and supplies to registered charities for use by the handicapped.

(5) **Advertisements:** This group still remains on the statute book as it was part of the 1983 Act. However, as of 1 May 1985, all advertisements placed in newspapers, periodicals and journals carry a VAT charge at the standard rate of 15 per cent.

(6) **News services:** This is an all-embracing group, as it includes most supplies and services to newspapers or news gathering organisations, except the supply of photographs.

(7) **Fuel and power:** Covering coal, gas, domestic heating oil, lubricating oil and the supply of electricity. The effect of this is that the heating of our households, as well as of our business premises, is zero rated. However, road fuels are taxed at the standard rate of 15 per cent affecting road haulage, which in turn increases business costs.

(8) **The construction of buildings:** Referring to both the construction of private homes as well as business premises, the freehold sale of your house or grant of your business lease for more than 21 years by a builder is covered by this zero rating. It also includes the demolition of buildings (a fact known to many businesses during the late 1970s and early 1980s when the industrial heartland of the UK was heavily hit by a depression) but not their repair. However, sales by builders merchants, and architect or surveyor's fees, remain taxable. Those 'do it yourself' individuals who propose to construct their own business premises (not merely make conversions or alterations) were brought into the standard rate VAT net, with effect from 31 May 1984.

(9) **Alteration, construction of any listed building:** This sub-category carries a zero rating and if you are in this business then you will be able to take full advantage.

(10) **International services:** Aimed at the 'Expatriate'. Professional advice to any individual working outside the EEC is charged at zero per cent. In some cases, the import of professional services can be liable to VAT. In general, but not exclusively, this item zero rates the export of services from the UK.

(11) **Transport:** No doubt many people in a wide variety of businesses will be interested in this category. Most forms of public transport are covered by this sector, including travel agents and international freight

Different types of VAT

transporters, but not businesses such as taxi firms, aircraft hire firms, car hire firms and pleasure cruises.

(12) **Caravans (excluding those used for holiday purposes) and house boats:** People who wish to live on rivers or taste a life of freedom on the roads are affected by this sector, including the manufacturers of these items. It must be a permanent abode to be classified under this sector and not merely used as a trailer on the road.

(13) **Gold:** Short but expensive, the supply of gold between the major banks and between the central banks and the London gold market are zero rated.

(14) **Bank notes:** The pound in your pocket is now worth 50p and luckily is not liable to VAT, otherwise it would be worth even less! The issue by a bank of a note payable to the bearer on demand carries no VAT.

(15) **Drugs, medicines, medical and surgical appliances:** If you are a pharmacist or a doctor, the medicines you dispense under prescription have no VAT element. However, any other drug purchased without a prescription must be charged at the full rate of VAT. This includes such items as aspirin, inhalers, etc, with the exception of medical and surgical appliances designed for the disabled. A manufacturer of wheelchairs for the disabled would be zero rated.

(16) **Imports and exports:** This group has limited application but provision is made for the zero rating of goods supplied before delivery, to avoid double taxation which would inflate business costs.

(17) **Charities:** The sale of donated goods in a charity shop, at a fête or coffee morning carries zero rating if that charity has been established for the relief of distress – and not your business either! Apart from this provision the sale of goods in a charity shop is treated in the normal way.

Where the branch of a charity makes business supplies, it may be treated as a separate entity from that charity subject to the limit of £21,300.

(18) **Clothing and footwear:** The last of our 18 categories affects the manufacturers and suppliers of children's clothes. It also includes those businesses which make and sell garments for use as protective wear.

We will now look more closely at our second category, those supplies which are exempt from VAT.

Exempt supplies

Zero rating has priority over exemption should goods or services fall into both categories. The following is a list of the major items of exemption, but further details are contained in VAT Notice 701.

(1) **Land:** This has been mentioned before but will be further clarified here. The granting of any interest or right over land is generally exempt. The sale or lease is also covered by this exemption, as an alternative to zero rating which can apply to the construction of new buildings or the reconstruction of listed buildings. However, hotels, holiday accommodation which includes camping sites, exhibition stands and sporting rights, remain taxable at the standard rate.

(2) **Insurance:** The provision of insurance of any description, together with the services of an insurance broker, are exempt. Therefore insurance premiums and the paying out on claims by an insurance company are exempt from VAT.

(3) **Postal services:** With the exception of telegrams, telephones and telex, the supply of postal services by the Post Office are exempt. However, the provision of these services by other private organisations does attract standard rate VAT.

(4) **Betting, gaming and lotteries:** Any charge on, for example, the playing of bingo, is exempt as are the services of a bookmaker. A subscription to a gambling club is liable to VAT, as are the takings from one-armed bandits etc.

(5) **Finance:** Banking services generally come within this exemption together with the supply of credit facilities. Stockbrokers' commissions, however, carry the standard charge, as do unit trust managers' fees. As from 1 May, 1985 the charges applied by credit and charge card companies to those outlets using their cards have become exempt, having previously been standard rated.

(6) **Education:** Schools, colleges, universities and other non-profit institutions providing education to pupils are exempt. This includes private tuition by an independent teacher. The effect of this exemption is to cover the provision of all educational facilities.

(7) **Health:** Doctors, dentists and registered opticians (including spectacles supplied in the course of treatment) together with chiropodists, dieticians, occupational therapists, physiotherapists, etc., are generally exempt. The only major exception would be charges for the use of a health farm.

(8) **Burial and cremation:** Undertakers' charges for dealing with funerals are exempt from VAT. However, a charge would be levied at standard rate on the provision of a tombstone.

(9) **Trade unions and professional bodies:** VAT does not apply on subscription to the above.

(10) **Sports competitions:** The cost of entering a sports competition, where the consideration is used wholly to provide prizes, is covered by this exemption.

(11) **Works of art:** When disposing of a recognised work of art in satisfaction of Inheritance Tax duties, no VAT is payable. It is worth remembering that where an item falls into the categories of both exemption and zero rating, the zero rating always carries priority.

Now that these two categories have been explained in detail you will know whether or not your business falls into the exempt or zero rated category.

3 Registration

Registration

It is most important for the small businessman to get his date of registration right, for if it is found that he should have been registered earlier than the date shown on form VAT1 (mentioned briefly in Chapter 1), he will still be liable to account for VAT on all the taxable supplies his business has made since that earlier date. Remember, it is the person, not the business, that is liable for registration. Thus, in principal, any person who at any time has reasonable grounds for believing that his future taxable turnover will exceed £21,300 in the current year must complete Form VAT1 and forward it to HM Customs and Excise.

It cannot be emphasised too greatly that the onus is on the individual who is carrying on the business to notify Customs and Excise and not vice versa. Not only may there be a considerable liability for arrears of tax, but in addition there are stringent penalties for failing to comply with this requirement and these will be dealt with in further detail at a later stage. The most common failure to register for VAT arises from a combination of not recognising all the taxable supplies the business is making, together with an oversight of the registration limits.

To assist the small trader in selecting his trade classification, which has to be entered at paragraph 4 on VAT1, in Appendix II we have reproduced a list of classification numbers from which the most appropriate selection should be made. When submitting your completed VAT1 to Customs and Excise you should state the date from which you had grounds for believing that you would be required to register under the 'at any time' proviso.

For the purposes of measuring taxable turnover, the tax exclusive value of any taxable supplies of goods, or the provision of services, is included. Please note that this will include all zero rated supplies, which we have already discussed. It does not, of course, include those items already defined as exempt supplies. There is no allowance made for the actual tax in determining the value for registration purposes.

Figure 1: Form VAT 1

H M Customs and Excise

VALUE ADDED TAX

APPLICATION FOR REGISTRATION

IMPORTANT

Before completing this form you should read the leaflet "Should I be registered for VAT?"

Use CAPITAL LETTERS, start at the beginning of each line and leave a space between words e.g.

MR JOHN MARK SMITH

FOR OFFICIAL USE

Date of receipt

1

Local office code and registration number

Name

Trade Name

Taxable turnover

E D R

D M Y

Stagger

Status

Rept. trader

Vol. trader

Oversize name ad...

Comp...

...oup

Intg. trader

Overseas trader

SPECIMEN

1. Full name of person or body to be registered

An individual should enter his/her title (e.g. Mr.) followed by first name(s) and surnames.

A company should enter its name.

A partnership should enter the firm name. If there is no firm name enter the full names of all partners. Form VAT 2 must b... completed.

2. Trading name if dif...

Enter the main trading ... different from the name wr... above.

3. Address of principal place of business

Give the address of the place where the day to day affairs of the business are dealt with.

Postcode

Telephone number ....

4. Trade classification

From trade classification booklet (VAT 41) select the four digit code number which most closely fits your main business activity and insert code number in box.

Trade classification

5. Expected turnover

See paragraph 3 of "Should I be Registered for VAT?"

What do you expect your total taxable turnover to be in the next 12 months? (Taxable turnover is the value of all supplies (sales of goods and services etc.) liable to VAT at the positive and zero-rates).

£ ....

6. Date of registration

See paragraph 6 of "Should I be Registered for VAT?"

Enter date from which registration for VAT is required

Enter date of first taxable supply (sales etc.) if different from above

Day Month Year

7. Bank account details

Enter for VAT repayment purposes **EITHER**

your Bank Sorting code No.

AND your Bank Account No.

OR your National Girobank Account No.

VAT 1

'F 3733 (Aug 1982)

Registration

Since its initial introduction on 1 April 1973, when the annual registration limit was only £5,000 per annum, to the most current increase to £21,300 effective from 18 March 1987 there have been a number of incremental increases as shown in Table 2.

Table 2: Incremental Increases

1 April '73	- 30 September '77	£5,000 pa
1 October '77	- 11 April '78	£7,000 pa
12 April '78	- 26 March '80	£10,000 pa
27 March '80	- 10 March '81	£13,500 pa
11 March '81	- 9 March '82	£15,000 pa
10 March '82	- 15 March '83	£17,000 pa
16 March '83	- 13 March '84	£18,000 pa
14 March '84	- 19 March '85	£18,700 pa
20 March '85	- 18 March '86	£19,500 pa
19 March '86	- 17 March '87	£20,500 pa
18 March '87	- onwards	£21,300 pa

The second proviso for registration of your business is, if at the end of any quarter, i.e. 31 March, 30 June, 30 September, 31 December, your past taxable turnover has exceeded £7,250 in that quarter or £21,300 in the last four quarters, you must again notify HM Customs and Excise office on Form VAT1. With effect from Royal Assent of the 1987 Finance Act the time allowed for such notification is increased from 10 to 30 days from the end of the quarter in which turnover reached the pre-set limit. The date to be entered at paragraph 6 of VAT1, under this proviso for registration, is the 21st day of the month following the end of the selected VAT quarter, that is 21 January, 21 April, 21 July or 21 October. If your requirements are satisfied by the 'at any time' provision or 'at the end of the quarter' provision then the date of registration is taken to be the earlier of the two dates.

You can, however, be registered at an earlier date than the one laid down by law. This will enable you to reclaim VAT suffered on pre-trading expenditure. Should the turnover of your business, however, be below these limits there is no statutory requirement to register. On the other hand, it may be to your advantage to register on a voluntary basis. To do this you must show that your business has a 'compelling business need'.

This could apply, for example, to a small unregistered business that finds itself at a disadvantage to larger registered businesses or if your supplies are zero rated. Registration would be beneficial to you since you would be able to reclaim your input tax, e.g. tax on business petrol, without having to charge output tax. It would also be beneficial to your fully taxable customers provided they were fully taxable at standard rate, since they would be able to reclaim the tax charged thereon.

HM Customs and Excise has made it clear that voluntary registrations will only be considered where the business concerned is that trader's sole livelihood and that the refusal of such registration would cause him to suffer the disallowance of a substantial amount of input tax. If voluntary registration is refused by Customs and Excise they must state their reasons in writing. It is then up to the trader to consider whether it is worth his while to lodge a formal appeal. We shall deal with these matters in greater detail in Chapter 11.

It is not always advantageous to be voluntary registered. In the case of a small businessman who is registered for VAT (e.g. a painter and decorator) with chiefly unregistered customers, ie private individuals, he would probably lose business since he would have to increase his prices to take VAT into account and his customers would be unable to reclaim it.

Even if you do not have to register at present, you should remember the limits defined as there may be a future increase in your taxable turnover which would make it necessary to register. You should remember that the taxable turnover is the value of and not the profit on all taxable supplies both standard and zero rated made in the UK and Isle of Man. This includes any supply which has been made by you but under a different business name, sideline activity, or goods acquired for private or non-business use, and amounts received in advance of making the actual supply.

If you have taken over a business from someone who is already registered, then you must take into account the level of taxable turnover made under the previous owner. Although you must notify Customs and Excise if your taxable turnover exceeds the figure of £7,250 in any one quarter, you do not have to be registered if you can satisfy the VAT office that your taxable turnover, including the quarter that has exceeded this figure, plus the next three quarters, will not exceed the figure of £21,300. This will be of particular importance to those seasonal trades already mentioned.

As soon as you know that you are required to be registered, in addition to notifying the office of Customs and Excise, you should start keeping VAT records (see Chapter 4) and you must also commence charging VAT to your customers. After submitting Form VAT1 you will be allocated a VAT registration number. Until this number has been allocated you must not show the tax as a separate item on any invoice. But if you are supplying your wares to customers who themselves are registered and who will want to claim the tax charged by you as an input against their supplies, you should explain to them that you will issue a VAT invoice in due course. The VAT invoice is described in Chapter 7.

Registration

If your business is a partnership, when applying for registration all the partners' names, addresses and signatures should be supplied on Form VAT2 as shown below.

Figure 2: Form VAT 2

	Value Added Tax		For official use
HM Customs and Excise	NOTIFICATION OF LIABILITY TO BE REGISTERED FOR VALUE ADDED TAX		Registration number

If the notification on Form VAT 1 is for a partnership, please list below, in BLOCK LETTERS, the full names of all the partners and their addresses.

This form must be signed by each partner in the space provided and forwarded together with Form VAT 1 to the Customs and Excise VAT office.

Any changes in the composition of the partnership must be notified to your local VAT office immediately.

Full name ....
Address
including
postcode ....

Signature .... Date ....

Full name ....
Address
including
postcode ....

Signature .... Date ....

Full name ....
Address
including
postcode ....

Signature .... Date ....

Full name ....
Address
including
postcode ....

Signature .... Date ....

Full name ....
Address
including
postcode ....

Signature .... Date ....

VAT 2   F 3736 (Sept, 1980)

SPECIMEN

It should be remembered that all the taxable supplies made by a person are aggregated to determine whether or not the registration limits have been exceeded and that all businesses are covered by a single registration. A partnership constitutes just such a 'person' and it is essential to differentiate between the supplies made by a particular partnership and those which are made by a separate, but possibly very similar trade.

The VAT paid on goods or services prior to registration is not strictly speaking an input tax for VAT purposes, although Customs and Excise will grant relief in the following circumstances.

(1) Goods including capital items and stock, that the business had obtained for its purposes and that were held as stock in trade as at the date of registration.

(2) Services that have been supplied for business purposes within six months of the date of registration but are not in respect of goods that have been solid prior to that date.

A person who is intending to make taxable supplies but at this moment is not yet doing so, could seek registration in advance. Assuming that this is granted by Customs and Excise, it would enable him to reclaim the input tax provisionally on the purchase he has made before he even starts to make taxable supplies himself. Before granting registration on this basis, Customs and Excise will always require firm evidence of the businessman's intention to trade. Specific regulations have been introduced which must be complied with when granting registration as an 'intending trader'.

(1) The input tax credit can only be allowed to the extent that it is wholly attributable to the intended taxable supply.

(2) The input tax must be repaid to the Customs and Excise at their request if it is not wholly attributable to a taxable supply or they are no longer satisfied that a taxable supply will be made. This input tax will be repaid if, for example, no taxable supply has been made within one year of registration.

All invoices in respect of input tax claims must be retained by the businessman for a period of six years.

Customs and Excise has the power to vary the conditions and impose specific conditions in individual cases but it is important for a person registering as an 'intending trader' to keep his position and the conditions under constant review until his registration is no longer conditional.

Early registration can, therefore, enable input VAT to be recovered which would otherwise be completely lost.

The person who completes the application form VAT1 will depend on the nature of the business. If you are a sole trader then it is you who signs the form. Where you are trading with another person in a partnership (but not a limited company) then any partner of the business may sign and apply. In the case of a limited liability company incorporated under the

UK Companies Act preferably the company secretary or any other director of the firm should sign the form. For an unincorporate association such as a sports club, an authorised official of the club signs. In the case of a trust then any of the trustees may sign VAT1.

Once you have made your application to your local VAT office and the Customs and Excise is satisfied that you are liable to be registered for VAT they will send you a preliminary advice notice of registration once your form has been checked. On this preliminary advice note will be shown your VAT registration number, which you must then at all times quote on any invoice sent out to customers.

If you are just starting out in business it is worthwhile waiting until this number has been sent to you officially before arranging for your business stationery to be printed. The preliminary advice note will also show your date of registration. Shortly afterwards a formal Certificate of Registration will follow showing your full registration details.

If you have applied for voluntary registration or for registration before you have made a taxable supply, i.e. you know the date when your business will commence and that your total turnover will exceed £21,300, you will only be given a registration number after Customs and Excise has accepted your registration. You will also be sent a number of publications from the VAT office including a VAT Guide Notice 700.

Businesses who apply for registration must ensure that full VAT accounting records are kept *from the date the VAT limit was exceeded*, not from the date of registration, and that they in turn have *charged out VAT* from that date. Even if you have not charged VAT on your invoices from that appropriate date, Customs and Excise will still demand this tax from you – a costly mistake should you have overlooked this procedure. However, you should bear in mind that you *cannot* show VAT as a separate item on your invoice until you have received your registration number. It is permissable, however, to adjust your prices to include VAT with an explanation to your customer that you will send the tax invoice at a later date. Having obtained the registration number you should issue the invoices within 30 days showing VAT due.

It cannot be stressed too often that businesses must keep an accurate and complete record of accounts showing VAT charged out on goods sold and VAT paid on goods received. Methods of accounts will be dealt with later in this book.

Thus, if you are registered for VAT you must keep records of all the supplies that you have made together with all the supplies you have received. These items are then consolidated into a summary for the last three months of trading, known as your VAT account. How to complete your VAT return is dealt with in Chapter 8.

Not everyone will maintain exactly the same records. In the majority of cases your invoices will form the basis of your records. For those of you who sell numerous small items direct to the public, for most of the sales you will find it is impossible to issue an invoice for each transaction. In turn, the public are not in a position to claim back the VAT included in your sale price and therefore do not usually want to have such proof of tax. This is why the retail schemes that we will be describing in Chapter 4 are available for adoption. If you are using a retail scheme you do not have to issue an invoice unless a customer specifically asks you for one. Remember, however, if you are asked for a VAT invoice, you are legally bound to give one to your customer.

A record must be kept of all the taxable goods and services that you receive or supply as part of your business including both standard and zero rated supplies. A separate record of the exempt supplies made by you also has to be started and maintained.

When recording your sales, if you issue tax invoices for all your standard rated sales and you also issue invoices for other sales that you make and the information shown on both is the same, then as long as you retain a copy of your sales invoices you need only make a summary for HM Customs and Excise. A summary (see the examples in Chapter 8) is maintained in the same order as your copy invoices. Separate totals are needed to show firstly the VAT on your sales, secondly the VAT *exclusive* value of what you have just sold, thirdly any exempt sales, fourthly the VAT due on any imports and finally, any credits you have allowed for your customers for return of goods.

Your VAT account is basically a summary of the totals of your outputs and inputs for each three month period (VAT quarter). At regular intervals it is essential to add up your totals under separate headings, as shown below.

Table 3: VAT Accounts

VAT Deductible (Input Tax)	VAT Payable (Output Tax)
Purchases	Sales
Imports (items purchased from overseas)	Exports (items delivered overseas)
Errors in previously submitted returns	Errors in previously submitted returns
Bad debt relief	
Allowable credit	Allowable debit

At the end of each tax quarter you subtract the total of your input tax from the total of your output tax and record the difference either owing to you or payable to HM Customs and Excise. This is dealt with at greater length in Chapter 8.

De-registration

De-registration is mentioned briefly here, but full details can be found in Chapter 12.

Registered traders can apply for de-registration when the value of their taxable supplies does not exceed certain limits. As from 1 June 1987 an application for de-registration can be made if the value of the taxable supplies is not expected to exceed the figure of £21,300 in the year that is just then beginning. The small businessman can also apply for de-registration when the value of his supplies in each of the two previous years has not exceeded the figure of £21,300 and it is unlikely to exceed a similar level in the year that is just about to commence. As from the date of the Royal Assent to the 1987 Finance Act the eligibility for de-registration will be based solely on future turnover. This should allow greater flexibility for the smaller trader such as a painter and decorator enabling him to reduce his costings when dealing only with unregistered customers, and thus perhaps become more competitive. The notification that a trade has ceased must again be made within a period of 30 days.

4 Selecting a scheme for your business

There are a number of retail schemes available which are for the use of everyone not just the corner shopkeeper who deals mainly with the public and who, for whatever reason, cannot issue a tax invoice for each sale. These schemes are designed to be used by the businessman who may make most of his supplies available direct to the public, but who may also have other retail outlets. This chapter contains a summary of the nine schemes currently in use, to give some idea of the points to be taken into consideration when choosing the right scheme for your business. Your local Customs and Excise office can supply more detailed information in the form of a number of publications in their Series 727, available either directly or by post. These schemes are summarised as follows and further details are given on the following pages.

(1) When using only standard rated goods Scheme A alone can be used.

(2) In respect of services provided, Schemes A, B and F are available.

(3) Schemes C, D and G are not available for supplies of catering, self-made or grown goods.

(4) Scheme C operates on fixed mark-ups which should be compared to the actual mark-ups on standard rated goods supplied. Should the fixed mark-ups be higher, a retailer would pay excess tax under the operations of Scheme C and would therefore be financially better off selecting another suitable scheme.

(5) When using Schemes E, G and H an opening stock take is required. In addition, Scheme J will require an annual stock take.

(6) In cases where the purchase price can easily be recorded but it is not quite so easy to determine the selling price, Schemes C, D and G should be considered.

(7) Schemes D and G will almost certainly result in more tax being due than any of the other schemes, if a higher mark-up is used for zero rated goods than for standard rated goods.

VAT - A working guide for the small business

The schemes are shown below in more detail and these should be read and considered in light of individual circumstances.

Scheme A

Probably the simplest scheme to operate and the most widely used, where all sales are at a standard rate of tax this scheme is applicable to businesses of any size. The output tax liability due to Customs and Excise can be simply calculated by using the VAT fraction of $3/23$rds applicable to the current standard rate tax of 15 per cent. The VAT fraction to be used when the price charged to your customers includes VAT is calculated as
rate of tax + rate of tax.
100

This is then multiplied by the gross takings recorded in any one period. For example, gross takings on 6 June of £7,000 × $3/23$ = £913.00. This can be cross checked by taking the balance of £6,087 and multiplying it by the standard rate of VAT, 15 per cent. By adding the two figures together the original turnover figure of £7,000 is found.

When using Scheme A you must keep a full record of your daily gross takings in respect of all the supplies covered by that scheme. The form in which you keep these records is a matter of personal choice, but you may find the model shown in Table 4 a useful guide.

You should keep with your records all the worksheets and copies of rough calculations you have made when working out your scheme output tax. This will save you both time and effort when the officers of HM Customs and Excise visit your business to verify that you have been operating the collection of VAT properly.

You will then need this output tax figure when compiling your VAT return (Form VAT 100), the completion of which is described in detail in Chapter 8.

Selecting a scheme for your business

Table 4: Retail Scheme A. Daily account for gross takings

Additions (a)							Subtractions (b)				
Date	Gross takings £	Value of goods for personal use £	Credit cards sales £	Value of tokens taken in exchange for goods £	Part exchange cash deduction £	Face value of debts sold on £	Refund on returned goods £	Value of tokens sold £	Trading stamp company charges £	Cash exchanged for own trading stamp £	Credit charges £
1.4.87	250.00	10.00	90.00	8.00	2.00	Nil	10.00	4.00	5.00	—	5.00
30.4.87	150.00	5.00	75.00	2.00	1.00	1.00	40.00	1.00	2.00	2.00	Nil
30.5.87	300.00	12.00	100.00	5.00	2.00	Nil	5.00	4.00	10.00	1.00	3.00
30.6.87	220.00	1.00	60.00	2.00	1.00	1.00	15.00	5.00	4.00	1.00	6.00
‡‡	‡‡	‡‡	‡‡	‡‡	‡‡	‡‡	‡‡	‡‡	‡‡	‡‡	‡‡
	22500.00	360.00	6300.00	180.00	90.00	10.00	1250.00	120.00	180.00	12.00	40.00

(a) Total of additions   29440.00
(b) Total of subtractions   1602.00
Gross takings (a–b)   27838.00

NOTE: Sample entries only shown above. There would normally be one entry per day on all takings throughout the three-month period.

Scheme B

This scheme remained unchanged in the recent 1987 Budget. However, the Chancellor has announced that there is a new scheme to be introduced. This will be known as Scheme B1 and will be an alternative to the existing Scheme B. A further complication is that there is yet another adaptation called Scheme B2 effective from 1 October 1987. Scheme B itself can be used in cases where the businessman makes supplies both at the standard rate (15 per cent) and zero rate and again, is applicable to businesses of any size. Using this scheme the selling prices of zero rated goods made for resale gives a zero rated taking. This is deducted from the total gross daily takings to arrive at a figure for standard rated takings against which the VAT fraction is applied to determine the amount of output tax liability. For example:

Daily gross takings	=	£10,000
Less expected zero rated taking	=	£ 1,300
Total	=	£ 8,700
VAT due 8,700 × 3/23	=	£ 1,185

When using Scheme B in relation to a service industry, any service supplied under its rules would have to be at the standard rate of tax and the takings from zero rated sales must not exceed 50 per cent of turnover.

Under the new scheme B1 there will be no 50 per cent rule, with no turnover restrictions but there will be an annual adjustment to stock levels.

Scheme B2 no longer has a fixed mark up of 14 per cent related to zero rated goods received for resale. Instead various fixed increased mark-ups will be applied based on the types of zero rated goods sold, together with the application of an annual turnover restriction of £500,000.

Scheme C

The annual turnover for this scheme was increased in the 1987 Budget to £90,000. Under this scheme both standard rated and zero rated supplies can be made but it cannot be used for the supply of services or for goods grown or made by a business. It cannot be used by a business even if it has a separate shop or department that in itself has a taxable turnover of £90,000 per annum or less. It is the total turnover of the whole business that counts, not just that particular outlet. Scheme C therefore cannot be used on, for example, the first £90,000 of taxable turnover. Basically this scheme works on the assumption that for most small businesses the goods that they receive for resale in a tax period are a reasonable measure of the goods that are sold in that period. This may be because they operate from a limited stock of goods which are replaced as they are sold. The stock that a retailer holds at the start of using Scheme C will, therefore, not enter into the scheme calculations. The three steps to follow in using this scheme are:

(a) You must add up the cost to your business, including VAT, of all the things you buy to sell in the trade at a positive rate.

(b) Then add on a fixed mark-up (See Appendix III) to each total. In this context the mark-up means the addition that is made to the cost price to arrive at your retail selling price. The Customs and Excise fix a single mark-up for each different kind of retail outlet.

(c) You multiply the total arrived at for each positive rate of tax by its own VAT fraction. The result is the output tax at that rate under Scheme C. For example

Cost (including VAT) of standard rated goods	£15,000
Mark-up (say 25 per cent)	£ 3,750
Cost plus mark-up	£18,750
Therefore VAT is £18,750 × $3/23$ =	£ 2,446

When using this scheme you will have to keep a record for each positive rate of tax with which you deal (currently there is only one positive rate, i.e. 15 per cent) and the total cost to you inclusive of VAT of all the goods that you receive for retailing. You will need to know the total costs of your zero rated purchases for each tax period when completing your VAT return (Form 100). Also you must keep a record of your daily gross takings.

Schemes D and G

These apply when both standard and zero rated supplies are made for businesses which now have a turnover limit of less than £500,000, including VAT. The lower annual turnover limit that once applied to Scheme G was abolished this year. However, the one-eighth uplift has remained unchanged. Schemes D and G cannot be used for cases of goods made or grown by the business or for the supply of services.

The schemes apportion gross takings on the standard and zero rated purchases of goods for resale, i.e. the cost of standard rated goods over the cost of goods at both rates times the daily gross takings for that tax period equals the deemed standard rated amount of sales on which the VAT fraction of $3/23$rds is applied. Businessmen should bear in mind that there is an annual adjustment that has to be made when using Scheme D. As your business grows and the taxable turnover exceeds £500,000 a year, if using any of these specialised schemes then you would normally have to choose another scheme. When using a retail scheme such as D you must continue to do so for a full VAT year before changing to yet another scheme.

Scheme E

This is based on projecting your standard rated purchases to their expected selling prices to arrive at a standard rated taking. To use this scheme, you must make standard and zero rated supplies of goods and it must be possible to calculate your rate of stock on hand at the beginning by doing a physical stock take (i.e. making a list of all your saleable goods). Should this stock take not be done, then the value of goods that have been received by you for resale in the preceeding three months would be used.

In order to calculate your VAT output for the first period, add up your expected selling price, inclusive of VAT, on the standard rated goods you have in stock. (This will be noted as A in the following formula.) Then add up the expected selling prices, inclusive of VAT, of all standard rated goods received *since* the commencement of the VAT quarter. (This is noted as B.) Add A and B and multiply the figure gained by the VAT fraction to arrive at your output tax.

> Example: VAT quarter to 31 December 1987
> Expected resale of stock on hand at 1 October 1987   £ 5,000 (A)
> Supplies during the quarter   £10,000 (B)
> £5,000 (A) + £10,000 (B) = £15,000 × $3/23$ = £1,956.52
> VAT due 31 January 1988 = £1,956.52

In the second and subsequent quarters you only need to calculate your expected selling prices inclusive of VAT.

> Example: VAT quarter ended 31 March 1988
> Total expected selling prices, inclusive of VAT   £12,000 (B)
> £12,000 × $3/23$ = £1,565.22 VAT due 30 April 1988

When arriving at A and B, the actual or average mark-up must be used for each class of goods. Basically, this means that you cannot use an overall average figure applicable to all the goods which you sell.

Scheme F

This scheme is relatively simple to operate once you have separated your standard rated and zero rated supplies at the point of sale. To do this, you would have to operate a separate or multi-total till in your business. In order to calculate the output tax for each VAT quarter, first add up the daily gross takings on your standard rated sales. To calculate the output tax you simply multiply the total by the VAT fraction as in Scheme A.

> Example:
> Daily takings on standard rated sales £300 × $3/23$ = £39.13

Schemes H and J

These schemes are extremely complicated and before deciding whether or not to adopt a calculation of VAT using either of them, do first talk to your local HM Customs and Excise office as well as your accountant.

Scheme H is based on apportioning your business's gross takings on the expected selling price of both zero rated and standard rated items received.

Scheme J is based on a retailer's trade for a full year which will commence on the first day of the first quarter of the year (i.e. VAT year from 1 April 1987 to 31 March 1988, first VAT quarter commences on 1 April 1987).

The equation to use when calculating Schemes H and J is as follows. These schemes apply when goods are supplied both at standard rate and zero rate but do not include services. The amount due is based on the difference between the gross takings of the expected selling price and the zero rated goods currently held for resale.

Expected selling price of standard rate goods ÷ expected selling price of goods at both prices × daily gross takings for VAT quarter = standard rated sales of goods at both rates.

Several different adaptions of Scheme J are available, for example a three monthly stock evaluation under which each tax period, i.e. 1 April 1987 to 30 June 1987, would stand on its own and there would be no annual adjustment required. A new leaflet shortly to be published by $\overline{\text{HM}}$ Customs and Excise will show you how to work out the different Scheme J adaptations.

The standard method of calculating gross takings are to remain unchanged at present. The Government have indicated in their 1987 Budget that after considering representations about the calculation of gross takings it will remain the same although it will form part of a later review. The use of retail schemes for non-retailers is to be withdrawn. Such businesses affected will need to consider whether or not to switch to the Scheme of Cash Accounting (due to be introduced on 1 October 1987). Cash accounting was introduced by the Chancellor on 17 March 1987 to lessen the tax liability faced by small businesses (i.e. businesses who have a turnover of below £250,000 per annum).

Under this scheme, VAT would be accounted for to HM Customs and Excise on the basis of Cash Paid and Cash Received. This will considerably improve a small businesses' cash flow situation as previously VAT became payable 30 days from the end of the quarter in which the invoice was issued irrespective of whether that invoice had been paid or whether the money was still owing. Small businesses who wish to adopt this scheme will be required to make a fresh application to their local VAT office.

Once approved, this scheme will remain in operation in your business for a minimum of two years. Once in the scheme you cannot switch out of it to another one. A leaflet published in May of this year and available from VAT offices will show you how this scheme operates.

In addition, the Chancellor announced a further optional scheme, Annual Accounting. This will be available to all businesses which pay VAT regularly and have been registered for a minimum of 12 months. However, the business must have an annual turnover of less than £250,000. Should you choose to use this scheme, you will only be required to make one VAT return per year as opposed to the four quarterly payments required at present. You would, however, make nine equal payments on account by direct debit followed by a tenth and final balancing payment. The scheme is not due to be introduced until the summer of 1988. Leaflets will be available from local VAT offices from June of this year and invitations to adopt this Annual Accounting Scheme are to be included in the VAT notes sent out to all registered traders in autumn of this year.

To help you decide which scheme is best suited for your business, use the flow chart opposite.

General Accounting for VAT

The purpose of maintaining VAT records is to record all operations in your business which will in turn affect the amount of VAT payable to, or reclaimable from HM Customs and Excise. Your records must also show all taxable (inclusive of all zero rated supplies) goods and services made in the course of your trade and in addition, to record all exempt and other supplies made. Your accounting system should also record all corresponding inputs at both positive and zero rates of tax and be able to record all exempt and other inputs. The maintenance of accounts together with other documentary evidence will be required for viewing by HM Customs and Excise to prove that you have operated correctly VAT inputs and outputs. In addition, these will be required when supporting your claim to the monies owed to you by HM Customs and Excise.

The maintenance of your records should, therefore, enable you to speedily, readily and accurately prepare your VAT return. Records and accounts must be kept up-to-date preferably on a weekly basis. There is a legal obligation for you to retain them together with all supporting documentation plus your audited accounts for a period not exceeding six years. (How to fill in your VAT return form is shown in Chapter 8.)

HM Customs and Excise are shortly to appoint independent consultants whose brief is to examine and report on the financial effect on small businesses of the current legal requirement to maintain VAT records for a minimum period of six years. The writer is of the opinion that there is at least a reasonable possibility that this report should lead to the number of

Selecting a scheme for your business

Figure 3: Flowchart: choosing a retail scheme
START HERE:

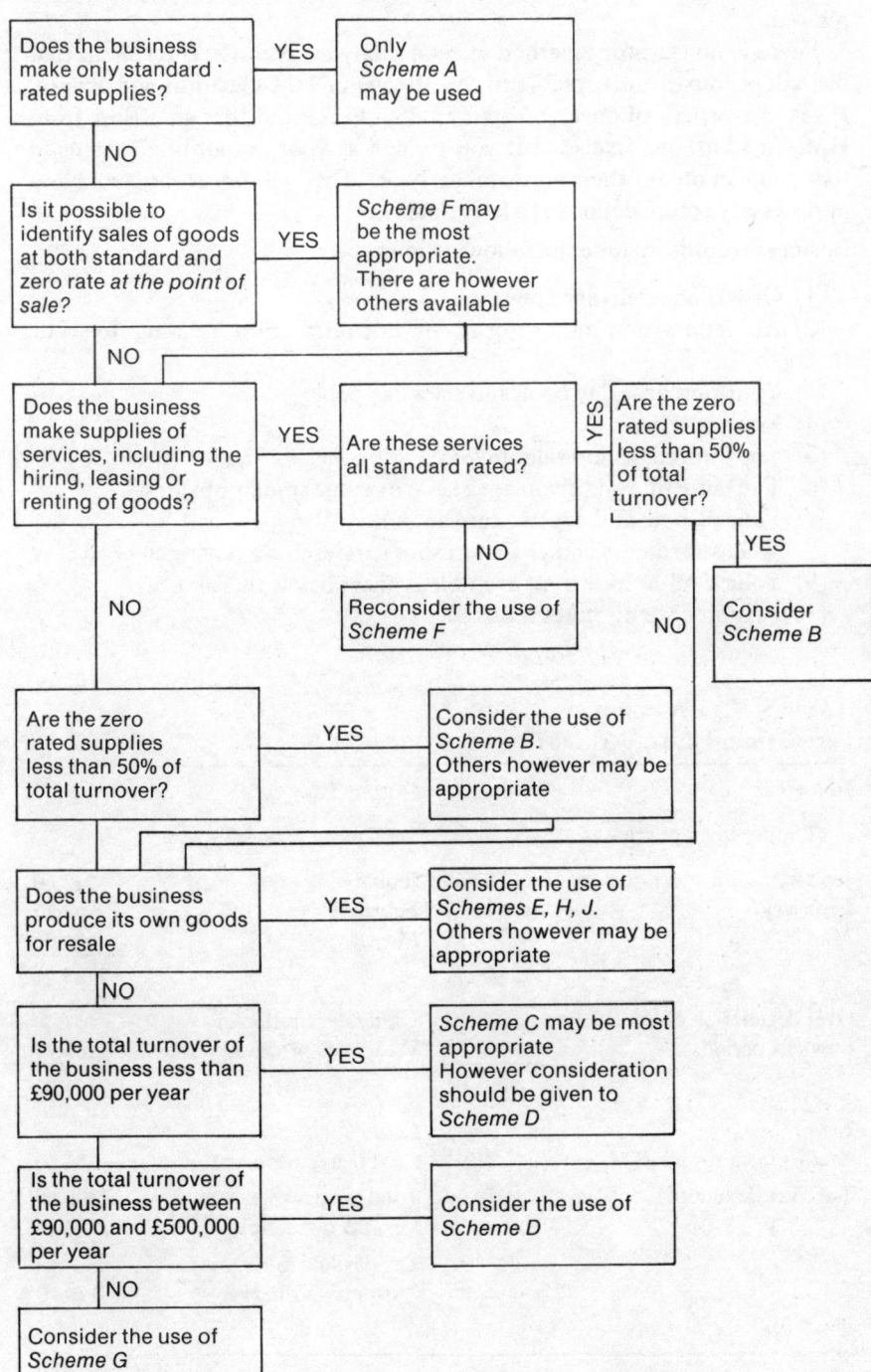

VAT - A working guide for the small business

rules and types of records currently required — to satisfy the, at times, overzealous Customs and Excise — being significantly reduced and relaxed.

There is no statutory method of retaining your records, the system that you adopt must be acceptable to the officers of HM Customs and Excise. It may be beneficial once you start trading to request that an officer from HM Customs and Excise visit you to look at your accounting system so that you can obtain their approval early on. This will hopefully avoid any unnecessary complications at a later date.

Business records include the following items.

(1) Orders and delivery notes.
(2) All letters and other forms of documentation relating to your business.
(3) Your purchase day book and sales day book.
(4) Your cash book.
(5) Copy purchase and sales invoice.
(6) The daily till roll (if you are a shop or run a similar business).
(7) Your income and expenditure accounts.
(8) Bank statements and paying in slips (preferably a paying in book).
(9) Your VAT account. An example is given below in Table 5.
(10) Credit or debit notes received.

Table 5: VAT Account
Period from 1.1.87 to 31.3.87

Input Tax	£	Output Tax	£
VAT suffered on purchases		VAT payable on sales	
January	782.60	January	912.00
February	841.20	February	967.15
March	518.11	March	606.06
	2141.91		2485.21
Over declaration of VAT from previous periods	150.00	Under declaration of VAT from previous periods	65.79
	2291.91		2451.00
Less		Less	
Credits from suppliers	21.91	Credits to customers	51.00
Total tax deductible	2270.00	Total tax payable	2400.00
		Less tax deductible	2270.00
		Tax payable to Customs and Excise	130.00

Larger businesses are permitted to use microfilm and computers to maintain their records provided that the information can be readily converted into a legible form upon request by HM Customs and Excise.

5 Input tax

As already mentioned cascade tax is essential in the collection procedure for VAT in that a taxable person is able to claim 'input tax' relief in respect of the tax charged on supplies of goods and services which have been made to him subject to the following items.

(1) A taxable person cannot claim input tax relief on the supply to him of any of these goods and services which are not going to be used for his business.

(2) Where the taxable person makes partially exempt supplies he cannot claim all the input tax against his outputs. For example, the use of a telephone with one quarter business use, showing VAT payable in that quarter of £100 would attract input tax restricted to one quarter, i.e. £25.

(3) Against certain expenses no input tax relief can be claimed at all, particularly on those items concerning the entertainment of UK customers and the purchase of private motor vehicles. However, when entertaining overseas customers, VAT incurred on entertainment *can* be reclaimed. An overseas customer is considered for tax purposes to be a person who is neither an ordinary resident (a person who does not live in the UK year by year) nor one who carries on a trade in the UK.

Business entertainment, where input tax is not deducted, is extremely wide ranging. It covers hospitality in any form even remotely related to the business. It does not include anything for bona fide members of your staff, for example, except where the provision for them is related to the provision of entertainment for other customers. Therefore this covers not only the obvious items such as meals, hotel accommodation, visits to football matches, etc, but goods and services such as leased use of aircraft, kitchen equipment and so on. If any capital goods have a dual purpose then again, like our telephone example, there is a restriction placed on the limit of the reduction.

Where input tax has been disallowed because the goods have been used for entertaining, there is a measure of relief as VAT is only levied on the excess of the selling price over the VAT inclusive purchase price. Surprisingly, where an employee plays host to guests at a restaurant while away on business, only applicable to the UK, the VAT in respect of his *own* meal can be reclaimed.

A taxable person's inputs are defined as being the goods and services that he obtains in the running of his business, included in these are the following items:

(1) Goods and services supplied to you in the UK.
(2) Goods imported by you into the UK.
(3) Goods that you have removed from a bonded warehouse for UK consumption.
(4) Certain services that have been received from outside the UK.

A taxable person is permitted to reclaim a deduction or a repayment on VAT returns in respect of the tax period during which the suppliers tax point has occurred as shown on his tax invoice. The tax invoice is described in detail in Chapter 7 and the completion of your VAT return is dealt with more thoroughly in Chapter 8.

Tax point

An area of extreme relevance when dealing with VAT is the matter of the date placed on invoices received by you, in order to reclaim VAT, i.e. what date (tax point) has been put against these goods? When you supply your business goods the *basic* tax point is the date which you send them to your customer or the date he physically removes these goods from your premises. Included here are supplies that you make under a hire purchase agreement, a credit sale or a conditional sale agreement (i.e. you have agreed to sell an item). However, if you do not send your goods away and they remain at your premises or are not taken away by your customer (for example, they are built on site), the basic tax point is the date they are made available for the customer's use.

For businesses that supply services, the basic tax point is the date on which the service is performed. This is not normally taken to mean the date on which all the work has been completed with the exception of the invoicing for that work. An example of this could be a consultant's invoice where work has taken place over, say, a two week period. The tax point would be the last day he attended to your business.

This basic tax point can be over-ridden by an *actual* tax point. The latter is when payment has been received before the supply of goods, i.e. a proforma invoice, or, the issue of your tax invoice up to 14 days after the supply of the goods. However, if you adopt the second rule, you must write and tell your local VAT office accordingly.

A tax invoice must actually be received by you in order for you to reclaim the input tax. It is not sufficient for a supplier to tell you that he has prepared an invoice, you have to actually receive it.

Using actual tax, a repayment claim or credit against your output tax can be deferred to a later tax period in cases where the tax invoice is still awaited (i.e. the 14 day rule). However, in cases where a tax invoice is received after the end of your VAT quarter, the input tax can still be reclaimed by you if the tax point (both basic and actual) has occurred within that quarter and you have not, as yet, submitted your VAT return.

Pre-registration input tax

If you have just started in business it is likely that you will have already incurred costs prior to the actual commencement date. Included in these costs there is almost certain to be an element of VAT on purchases made. Strictly speaking, VAT incurred before you have registered is not an input tax. However, HM Customs and Excise do permit under certain conditions for the VAT already paid to be reclaimed when submitting your first VAT return.

Your claim must be supported by the relevant invoices as proof of purchase together with any other evidence showing that VAT has been paid. In the case of goods, if you are a taxable person then you are permitted to treat as input tax any tax paid on the supply of goods to you prior to the date from which you were required to have been registered, provided that those goods were for the purpose of your business. However, those goods must not be disposed of prior to the date of your registration.

A separate stock account should be compiled and maintained for the period of time prior to the registration as you may have to submit this as proof to the HM Customs and Excise inspector. This stock account should show clearly the goods purchased, as shown in the example below, the date of purchase, the manner in which this merchandise was disposed of, and the date of disposal.

Table 6: Stock Account

Item	Quantity	Date of Purchase	Sold to	Date
Filing Cabinet	2	6.5.87	Jim Nastik	8.8.87
Typist Chair	6	18.5.87	K. Smith	22.7.87
Desk	1	4.6.87	B. Jones	6.6.87

In the case of services, it is allowable to treat as input tax any VAT on the supply of services to you before you have actually registered for VAT. As an example, Ken Smith owns and runs a small electrical retail shop. He decides to commence his business on 1 April 1987. During March 1987, however, he acquires a secondhand washing machine (not in working order) as part of his stock. He then has to employ a service engineer to repair it. This engineer charges £30 for his time, but since he is registered for VAT he also has to charge £4.50 VAT. He has provided a service to Ken and as long as Ken sells that machine on or after 1 April 1987 it will be in order for him to reclaim the £4.50 VAT he was charged as part of his input tax.

A further condition relating to this type of situation is that the service (in our example the repair to the washing machine) must not have been carried out more than six months prior to the date of registration (i.e. before 1 October 1986). As with goods, you should maintain a comprehensive list of the date of purchase and date of disposal in relation to these services.

In the majority of cases your suppliers' tax invoices will provide you with all the details needed in order to calculate your input tax. Therefore, you need only make a summary of the invoices and maintain them in the order you received them. It is advisable to number these invoices in sequence so that you can record the same number against the entries in your summary. This makes for ease of accounting.

It may also be possible to adapt your cash book to serve as a summary of your purchases in cases where you wish to deduct input tax at the same time as you pay your suppliers. Your summary must show separate totals as indicated by the following four points.

(1) The VAT you have been charged on your purchases.
(2) The VAT exclusive values for your purchases.
(3) The VAT due on any imports you may have.
(4) Any credits you may have received from your suppliers. (A credit received from a supplier can include an element of VAT which will serve to reduce the amount of tax which you are permitted to deduct from your output liability.)

A separate record should be kept in respect of those business purchases on which it is not permitted to deduct input tax, for example entertaining UK customers. Before transferring this VAT figure to your VAT account, you must first have a proper tax invoice and the nature of the purchase must have been related to your business purchases.

A proper tax invoice must carry your suppliers VAT number, full address, and itemised details of the purchase. Your own tax invoices should also contain this information. Examples of this are to be found in Chapter 7. Appendix IV details the method you use to determine whether or not your supplier has presented a genuine VAT registration number to you.

From 1 April 1987 a somewhat major upheaval in the input tax deduction rules has taken place which is of vital importance to the small business. It effects even those businesses which have hitherto not suffered any loss of tax. These tax changes basically mean that the making of VAT exempt supplies can have enormous financial consequences. The 'standard exemption method' has been completely remodelled.

For VAT quarters beginning on 1 April 1987 any partially exempt businesses will have to directly attribute between a taxable and exempt supply the appropriate input tax that has been incurred. In other words, before 1 April if you ran a small school and opened it up for the summer holidays for accommodation, providing camping facilities etc. (on which VAT was charged) and sold items including chocolates, drinks, milk and such like (on which again VAT was charged) you would have been able to reclaim all VAT charged on your purchases. For example, sales of your quarterly exempt supplies may amount to £1,000 and your chargeable supplies to £4,000 but you could reclaim input tax against the full £5,000. Now, however, the amount you will be able to reclaim is based directly on the amount of your taxable sales, ignoring any exempt supplies – such as school fees – you may have made. In the example used above you would now only be able to claim back tax on the £4,000 shown in your output sales.

This attribution is not a straightforward exercise but is complicated as it requires a business to relate specific sales to costs incurred in generating these sales. From 1 April it will only be possible to obtain a credit in respect of those purchased items which are directly linked to any VAT charge included in their cost to you.

Any residual tax which cannot be attributed one way or another will now only be able to be credited under a very complex formula which will involve small businesses in complicated calculations and procedures. You would be well advised if this does affect your business to seek professional advice.

Prior to the 31 March 1987, under the so-called *de-minimus* rule, provided your exempt supplies did not exceed one per cent of the value of your total supplies, they could be ignored for VAT purposes in calculating the amount of allowable input tax. This rule was designed basically to save as many registered traders as possible from the inconvenience of having to do partial exemption calculations, and as a result many businesses fell outside of the partially exempt net. Now this has all changed.

A partial exemption is a complicated area outside the scope of this book, but basically the workings of VAT have to recognise that a taxable person is making a variety of supplies, some of which are exempt from tax, some of which carry zero rating and others which are taxed at the standard rate of 15 per cent. If your business made only exempt supplies then by definition you are not making taxable supplies so you would not be eligible for registration. In turn you would be unable to claim back input tax relief.

Where a business is making exempt, standard and zero rated supplies, the problem arises as to how much of your input tax you can reclaim credit for when you are making some exempt supplies. For example, in the

VAT – A working guide for the small business

simplest of cases you would measure the relative mix of exempt and taxable supplies and then claim relief in the same ratio that the taxable supply bears to total supply. In other words:

Value of exempt supplies	£2,000
Value of taxable supplies	£4,000
Total supplies	£6,000

Therefore fraction of allowable Input Tax is two-thirds

Input tax, say	£ 900
Allow two-thirds of £900	£ 600

However, as from 1 April, only where a person's input tax attributable to exempt supplies in any period is less than a maximum of £500 per month on average, or 25 per cent of all input tax, then all input tax incurred may be recovered.

The depressing news for UK businesses is that the changes mentioned above will increase the UK VAT intake by some £300 million in the financial year ending 31 March 1988. There is little question that the bulk of this revenue will be extracted from those businesses that up until 31 March 1987 had escaped from the clutches of partial exemption.

In addition, in terms of non-productive time devoted to acting as unpaid tax collectors, which all businesses who operate the VAT are, even those small businesses whose exempt related inputs still fall within the *de-minimis* rules will be required to do the direct attribution calculations on a constant basis, if only for their own peace of mind with regard to their trading position, in that it has not exceeded the new regulations. It has therefore become essential for all small businesses, especially those who have large amounts of exempt related inputs, which were in the past sheltered by the old *de-minimis* rules to closely and critically examine their trading position so that the maximum of £500 per month exempt level is not exceeded. Again, consultation with your tax consultant is recommended.

6 Output tax

An individual who makes or intends to make goods or offer services in the UK other than an exempt supply is termed as a taxable person, and as such is required by law to charge VAT on all the positive rated taxable supplies of goods or services which that business has made in the UK in the course of its business. This type of Value Added Tax is known as Output Tax. It becomes the liability of the person or business who is making the product or offering the service, or indeed selling the firm's goods to charge output tax. Then it is the taxable person's responsibility i.e. yours, to pay over the tax which has been collected. You become, in effect, a non-paid tax collector on behalf of HM Customs and Excise.

In theory output tax becomes due at the time of the supply of the good(s) or service(s), but in practice it is accounted for and paid over to the Government by way of a VAT return for prescribed accounting quarters.

The two rates of output tax currently consist of a standard rate of VAT at 15 per cent and a zero rate of VAT. In calculating the amount of standard rate of output tax, the VAT fraction is used, as shown. This fraction is liable to change depending upon the rate of the tax, currently, it is $3/23$rds.

This is calculated as follows:

$$\text{VAT fraction} = \frac{\text{rate of tax}}{100 \text{ plus rate of tax}}$$

Taking the current standard rate of tax of 15 per cent the VAT fraction applied is:

$$\frac{15}{100+15} = \frac{15}{115} = \frac{3}{23}$$

For example, suppose your total sales in the quarter ending 30 June 1987 amounted to £30,000 then the VAT on this amount is calculated as follows:

£30,000 × 3/23rds = £3,913.04

To cross check that your calculation is correct, take £30,000 and subtract the VAT from that, which is £3,913.04. The net sales, excluding VAT, would then equal £26,086.96. VAT at 15 per cent on this figure would be £3,913.04 thereby confirming that your initial calculation was correct.

It has been previously stated that VAT is charged on the supplies of goods or services made in this country. This in turn leads us to ask the question 'what is termed as a supply?' The EEC Sixth Directive dictates that the 'supply of goods' means that it is the 'transfer of the right to dispose of tangible property as owner'. In addition, the 1972 Finance Act gives further clarification in that 'anything which is not a supply of goods but is done for a consideration is a supply of services'. What it basically means is that there is no taxable supply if there is no cash transaction (except in certain circumstances which will be noted on page 52). For example, there is no VAT payable on wages or salaries because these payments are made as a result of a contract of service between employee and employer and *not* a contract of *services*. Similarly, there is no VAT payable on donations because you, as the giver or donor, receive nothing in return for this 'gift'.

There are a number of transactions which are considered to be a supply for the purpose of VAT, even though you may not recognise them as such in the normal course of business transactions. These are as follows:

(1) **Supplies to yourself:** Where goods, including those goods which have been manufactured by your business, are put to private use outside of this business. For example, if you are a washing machine manufacturer and a friend has the use of one of your products, this is considered to be a supply of goods despite the fact that there has been no cash exchange given for the use of those goods. Output tax still becomes due and payable on the notional cost of the supply.

This is an often forgotten section and one which can cause a problem as it is left off the quarterly returns only to rear its head later on when additional output tax is added to your returns by the Inspector during one of his routine visits. The objective of this legislation is to prevent the distortion of competition within the business community.

(2) **The free supply of services:** Although legislation does exist which enables the Treasury to prescribe the free supply of services which are chargeable to tax, to date no such order has been made. Consequently, in very broad terms, the free supply of services are not chargeable to VAT. Let us suppose that your brother is a solicitor and conveys your house

free of charge. Provided he does not levy a cost on you for this, he does not have to charge VAT on the notional value of his costs of the conveyance.

(3) **Gifts:** In instances where you give away items or these items are otherwise disposed of without cash being charged by you, provided that they no longer form part of your stock in trade, then VAT becomes chargeable. A gift is considered to be an item where you the donor, as the giver, is not obliged to give it away and the receiver of the gift is not obliged to do anything in return for this gift.

Goods costing less than £10, given away in the course of your normal business transactions, are exempt from this provision – as are all free meals to employees, and samples that are not normally available for sale to the general public. Otherwise, the cost of the supply is the full cost to you – the business – excluding VAT, and your profit margin. Thus, chargeable items include the price paid for each item plus any related costs, such as insurance, transport, or repair and in the case of goods you have manufactured, in addition to the basic material costs, all of your labour and overheads, such as heat and light.

This legislation now includes the private use of motor vehicles. Prior to 5 April 1987 you had to negotiate with your local HM Customs and Excise Inspector, a restriction on your input tax on such items as petrol, repairs, etc. This is based on your private mileage in relation to your annual mileage. This restriction, in most cases, was the same as the proportion of running expenses added on to your taxable profit by the Inspector of Taxes when dealing with your accounts. However, in respect of all accounting periods that start after 6 April of this year, a new simplified system applies to VAT on motoring expenses incurred by your business and as of this date, now affects your output tax. You must now account for VAT on:

(a) road fuel used for private motoring.
(b) charges for the use of a vehicle.
(c) motor cars sold by your business if the selling price exceeds the purchase price.

A business journey is defined as one made by you or your employees for the purpose of your business. By contrast, a private journey is defined as any journey made not for the purpose of your business. Therefore, travelling between your home and business location is classed as private motoring. If you employed a sales representative who spent most of his time travelling, the mileage incurred going into the office would be considered private while the remainder of the mileage incurred to collect orders, visit customers, etc. would be deemed as business.

You must account for VAT on fuel used for private motoring. Where your employee has a car for business use and petrol is put in for business purposes but in fact he uses the car for pleasure, then the private mileage is known as free fuel, and this also has to be accounted for. This output tax is

VAT – A working guide for the small business

calculated by using scale charges which will already be well known to company directors and employees earning more than £8,500 per annum (current rate), as they are the same scale charges used to calculate benefits in kind for tax purposes. These scale charges are given below and show the value of the fuel including tax.

The scale is applicable to a mileage per quarter of 4,500 (1,500 per month) or less. If more than four 500 miles are driven each quarter for each vehicle, then reduced scale charges apply.

Table 7: Standard Scale of Charges per Quarter

Cylinder Capacity	Scale of Charge	VAT due per Vehicle
Up to 1400cc	£120	£15.65
1401–2000cc	£150	£19.56
Over 2000cc	£225	£29.34

Table 8: Reduced Scale Charges per Quarter if Business Mileage exceeds 4,500

Cylinder Capacity	Scale of Charge	VAT due per Vehicle
Up to 1400cc	£60	£7.82
1401–2000cc	£75	£9.78
Over 2000cc	£113	£14.73

Note. If, however, you pay for all petrol with regard to your own private use, these charges do not apply. Should you only use your business vehicle for the occasional private journey it now pays you to fund the private mileage out of your own pocket – this applies whether you are a company director, a sole trader or in a partnership. In addition, you will not have to account for VAT if you do not allow any of your employees to use company cars for private motoring free of charge.

These scale charges and the resulting amount of VAT which has to be accounted for in respect of fuel, should be included in Box 1 of your VAT return form, as shown in Chapter 8.

(4) **Cancellation of registration:** On ceasing to be a taxable person, tax is chargeable on all the assets you have in stock at the time of de-registration unless the tax on this 'deemed' supply is not more than £250. Therefore, in most cases VAT applies.

There are a number of transactions which are considered not to be a supply for VAT purposes, these are summarised as follows:

(a) the transfer of a business as a going concern – a business still trading;

(b) the disposal of repossessed goods or those goods taken in settlement of an insurance policy claim;

(c) goods which you can prove have been lost or destroyed.

(5) **Time of supply:** It will not have escaped your notice that in calculating the relevant amount of output tax, which needs to be paid over to Customs and Excise, you must first establish the time of supply in which your goods or services were sold. In the supply of goods, the time of supply is seen to be the earliest of the following:

(a) the time the goods are removed from your premises;
(b) the date the goods are first made available to your customer;
(c) the date on which your invoice showing VAT is issued;
(d) the date on which payment is received in respect of the relevant supply.

These points do not apply if you elect to go on cash accounting. However, do remember that this facility can only be applied for if your turnover is below £250,000 per annum. In the context of (d), a returnable deposit does not constitute a payment.

If the invoice showing VAT is issued within a 14 day period of the 'basic tax point' in the instances of (a) or (b), then the date when your invoice is actually issued is substituted for the date of the entire supply. By applying to HM Customs and Excise this 14 day rule may be extended at their discretion and could be granted if it is not practical for you to issue an invoice within 14 days.

Should articles be sold on a sale or return basis, the basic tax point is taken to be the earliest of:

(a) the time when the customer purchased the goods;
(b) twelve months after the date when the goods were first despatched;
(c) or finally, in instances of a time period being less than twelve months, then the expiry of an agreed time limit, i.e. six months.

When services are supplied, the basic tax point is considered to be the date of the completion of the contract unless an invoice including VAT has been issued prior to the completion. In this instance, the date of the invoice's tax point becomes the date of supply.

The time of supply of goods for private purposes is deemed to be the date when those goods are actually used.

Place of supply

As United Kingdom VAT only applies to supplies made here, it is important to ascertain the *actual* place of supply. Naturally, goods that are already in this country and are not sold to go overseas are treated as being supplied in the UK. Goods that are exported are still regarded as being supplied in the UK but they will carry zero rating. This enables exporters to reclaim all their input tax incurred in the manufacture of these items.

Before HM Customs and Excise repay this input tax, there must be clear evidence that the exported goods have, in fact, been shipped overseas. It has been known in the past for exporters to claim that goods had left the UK when in fact they had not. One company filled shoe boxes with bricks and exported these so-called goods! Over a number of years they reclaimed a considerable amount of input tax before they were found out and heavily fined.

Penalties are indeed high for this type of fraud. In cases where goods are claimed to have been exported but subsequently found to be still in the UK, they are liable to be forfeited immediately and VAT charged forthwith to the person who is either in possession of the goods or by any other person who is found to be in possession of the goods in the UK.

If a supply of goods takes place outside the UK and those goods never actually enter the country, they are clearly outside the grasp of UK VAT net. However, if they are subsequently imported into the UK, they become liable to VAT unless the goods are held in a Freeport. Once they leave that Freeport VAT has to be paid.

In the case of services being supplied, the place of supply is seen to be the location of the service's office(s). However, should the company have two or more locations, the place of supply is deemed to be the location where the supply of services has been given. In the case of a private individual the place of supply is seen to be his home. And in the case of a registered limited company, the place of supply is the address of its registered office, regardless of the number of sub-offices it may have. A group of companies can elect to make just one VAT return covering all companies within that group from one address, usually the registered office of the main holding company. This VAT election has the advantage that no tax has to be accounted for when making supplies between member companies.

Value of supply

In the majority of cases, you will receive cash in exchange for your goods. The value of these items is taken to be the amount inclusive of VAT, which should equal the total of the value of goods supplied. Anti-avoidance provisions operate in instances where the supplier and the purchaser may be connected, i.e. father and son, husband and wife, etc. In such cases the market value of the goods supplied is substituted. This refers only to goods (manufactured items or items sold) and not services.

If you offer a discount as part of the terms of your business to encourage prompt payment, the value of your supply on which VAT is calculated is taken as the discounted price and *not* the full price, even if the discount is not actually taken. This is an interesting point and one which could well be noted by small businesses registered for VAT.

There are also special rules which govern the value of long-term accommodation by individuals in hotels. For example, should an elderly relative stay in an hotel on a long term basis, which is any time over 28 days, then VAT is no longer charged on the accommodation as it is considered to be rental. Before the change, businesses who held block bookings on hotel accommodation for their staff could gain VAT relief. However, these provisions no longer cover business accommodation and VAT is charged no matter how long the stay.

7 The VAT invoice

One of the most important business accounting documents you should have in your possession is the VAT invoice. It is your proof of your customer's claim for the tax deduction you have charged him and, provided he is registered, will have been added into his input tax against his own liability.

You, as a supplier, need to retain a copy of *all* your invoices as part of your VAT records (and, needless to say, your business records) and likewise your customer will need to retain the top (or original) copy as proof of tax paid. Invoices cannot be prepared on the assumption that one day they will be collected. An invoice is only considered for taxable purposes if *it has been posted or given to an individual or person representing a business to whom it will be paid*. It is advisable to keep a record of all invoices issued and received for a period of at least six years.

You are legally bound to give a tax invoice whenever you supply standard rated goods or services to another registered taxable person. The one exception to this rule is where your customer operates an HM Customs and Excise approved self-billing arrangement (see page 58).

An important point to watch out for, is that if you receive an invoice which has VAT added on to it from a trader who is not registered then not only is the tax payable to Customs and Excise by the person issuing the invoice, but you, as the receiver of this bogus invoice, cannot claim credit for the tax shown as an input. See Appendix IV on how to tell whether a VAT registration number is bogus or not.

A tax invoice does not need to be given to customers who are not registered for VAT, unless, of course, they ask for one, in which case you have a legal duty to supply them with a copy.

Your tax invoice should be presented within 30 days after the basic tax point (covered in Chapter 6) in the case of single supplies, unless HM Customs and Excise otherwise allow. In the case of a continuous supply (management service business who supplies invoices every month over a period of, say, six months for an ongoing service), it has to be presented

VAT – A working guide for the small business

within 30 days of the event which creates the tax point, in other words the date when the bill is issued. In certain circumstances the issue of the tax invoice itself, as mentioned earlier in this book, can create the tax point.

Invoices showing VAT must not be issued to individuals or businesses who are paying for the items *if* the goods are being delivered to another source. Tax can only be reclaimed by the person to whom the goods are being delivered. If the error is yours then you cannot set the tax charged against your tax liability (output tax).

Table 9: Example of a tax invoice.

Sales Invoice No. 201   VAT Reg. No. 12398751

Fly by Nite Bros.,
Lawn Turf Supplies,
Rookham Lane,
Cheetham

Tax point: 7/9/87
To: Mr. I. Trustham,
    School Lane,
    Wareham

Quantity	Site	Price	Amount	VAT
100 sq. yds. of lawn turf	Abbey End playing fields	50p per sq. yd.	£50	£7.50

TOTAL DUE   £57.50

Let us look at this example in more detail. The statutory requirement insists that a tax invoice must contain the following information.

(1) **An identifying number.** An invoice number must be shown on each invoice issued. For your accounting purposes this should be in sequence so that no number is duplicated and sales invoice numbers given can be seen in date sequence too.

(2) **Date of supply.** This is the time when the supply of goods or services is treated as having taken place.

(3) **Your name, address and registration number.** These details pertain to you, the supplier, and must show your full trading name, full address and registration number given to you by the Customs and Excise (you will recall that this number is exclusive to you).

(4) **Name and address of purchaser.** This point has been covered above. However, to reiterate, the full name and address of the person who receives the goods must be shown on your sales invoice.

(5) **The type of supply according to categories.** This refers to the type of transaction under which the invoice is raised, i.e. lease, hire purchase, cash transaction, etc. The different types of supply are:

(a) Supply by sale, which covers the majority of transaction, for cash consideration.

(b) Supply by hire purchase, which covers any item supplied, such as caravan, car, boat, etc, from which you receive a deposit from the purchaser and the balance from a finance company.

(c) Supply by loan, which covers informal arrangements between you and your customer, i.e. he can take delivery of your goods before payment is made over an agreed period of time.

(d) Supply by lease or rental, which covers any item supplied, such as television and videos, whereby ownership is retained by you and does not pass to the individual who possesses them.

(e) Supply of goods made by customers' materials, which covers any material or item supplied and the customer makes a request for it to be made into an item. An example would be a registered dressmaker who makes clothes for a fashion outlet. This outlet brings the material and the design pattern for him/her to make up. The dressmaker would charge for his/her time and VAT would be levied on this charge.

(f) Supply by sale on commission, such as purchases made at a tupperware party.

(g) Supply on sale or return basis. This has already been covered and is self-explanatory.

(h) Supply especially introduced by HM Customs and Excise to cover 'catchall' situations which they apply at their discretion.

(6) **Description of goods or services supplied.** This has to identify clearly, the items sold or the services supplied, i.e. one video, one washing machine.

(7) **Description.** For each description shown, the details must include the quantity of the goods or the extent of the services, the rate of tax applicable giving the amount payable, excluding VAT, in pounds sterling, for example, 20 LPs at £5.00 each.

(8) **Total.** The total amount payable excluding VAT given in pounds sterling. Using the example shown here, the LPs have a total cost of £100.

(9) **Rate.** The rate of any cash discount given. In other words, if you give a discount, then this has to be clearly shown, i.e. less 5 per cent.

(10) **Amount.** The amount of VAT chargeable at each rate. This is a legacy from earlier days when luxury goods carried a higher rate. For all purposes there are currently two rates of VAT, zero rated and standard rate at 15 per cent.

(11) **Total charged.** The total amount of VAT chargeable again expressed in pounds sterling. In the case of our LPs this would be £15, i.e. £100 × 15 per cent.

If either zero rated or exempt goods are included on this invoice then they must be shown clearly as separate totals as no VAT is levied against them; the invoice must show that the items have no VAT added on them.

VAT – A working guide for the small business

It will be common in retailing for the final consumer to be a member of the public who will, of course, not be registered for VAT. As they are not in a position to reclaim the tax charged them, they will either not require an invoice at all or simply just ask for a receipt as proof of payment for the items purchased. However, should a member of the public ask for a tax invoice, provided that the value of the goods supplied does not exceed £50 inclusive of VAT, a much less detailed tax invoice may be given. This modified invoice need only contain the following information:

(a) your name, address and registration number;
(b) the date of sale;
(c) sufficient description to identify the transaction;
(d) the total amount payable inclusive of tax;
(e) the rate of tax chargeable (presently there is one rate and this is at 15 per cent).

Table 10: Modified Tax Invoice

	The Bee Tea Room 24 High Street New Beaton	
VAT No. 867340		1st May 1987
Item	Price	Total
2 Lunches	£5.50	£11.00
	VAT 15%	£ 1.65
		£12.65

Unless prior approval has been obtained from HM Customs and Excise, when using a modified tax invoice you should not include items which carry a zero rate of VAT or are exempt from the reaches of VAT altogether.

Under certain conditions, when a supply exceeds £50 inclusive of VAT and your customer is agreeable, instead of showing the tax inclusive value and a description of each item separately you may show at the bottom of the invoice the following:

(a) the total amount of the goods purchased including the VAT payable at any one rate;
(b) the total amount of tax payable at that rate;
(c) the total value exclusive of VAT.

Again, it is allowable for zero rated or exempt supplies to be shown but separate totals must be clearly identifiable.

Depending upon the nature of your business, provided HM Customs and Excise have given written approval, it may be possible for you, as the customer, to make out your own tax invoice as though you were the supplier, provided your supplier is registered for VAT. This self-billing

The VAT invoice

system is not widely used except in certain businesses such as the construction and related trades and businesses involving the payment of royalties, for example the publishers of this book. The operation of this system can have its disadvantages and give rise to areas of confusion. As a word of warning, should you be using or thinking of using this system, all invoices prepared under this self-billing system should show clearly the following endorsement: 'The tax shown is the amount of output tax now due and payable to HM Customs and Excise'.

This system would probably be used in cases where the consumer not only has the basic information necessary to complete the invoice but may be in a position whereby his/her accounting facilities are more sophisticated administratively than the actual suppliers. In making the application to your local branch of HM Customs and Excise, the following information will be required by you:

(a) a detailed description of the proposed system;
(b) valid reasons for its adoption;
(c) written agreement from the supplier for its adoption.

However, it is important for you to ensure that the supplier has not, under any circumstances, issued his own invoice in connection with these transactions, in other words duplicated them. Should you operate this system or think of applying for its adoption, a word of warning; it is up to you to clarify that not only is your supplier registered for VAT but during the course of your trading relationship with him that he continues to be registered. If for some reason your suppliers registration is cancelled, you as the customer need to be notified so that you can in turn cease to apply VAT on the relevant and subsequent transactions.

During the course of your transactions, it may be necessary to issue a proforma invoice in respect of goods or services offered to potential customers. Subsequently, these goods or services may not be taken up by the customer.

A proforma invoice will often have the same amount of information as the standard tax invoice. To avoid this confusion a proforma invoice should carry the following wording: 'This is not a tax invoice'. Unless this is made clear on the invoice, it may result in the customer claiming input tax when he is not entitled to.

Once the potential offer or supply of goods is accepted a bona fide tax invoice should be issued under your normal accounting administration.

In our electronic age, it is possible to transmit invoice details via a computer. HM Customs and Excise is agreeable to accepting the transmission and receipt by a computer provided you have satisfied them of your method of recording. Before introducing a computerised system such as this, you should write to HM Customs and Excise giving one calendar month's notice before introducing it as they may lay down certain conditions applicable to your business when authorising the use of your particular system.

8 VAT Returns

When you first register for VAT you will be allocated an accounting period by the Customs and Excise office. This period will be on a three-monthly basis. However, the initial period may be in excess of three months, depending upon the date you first registered because HM Customs and Excise need to stagger the periods. These three month tax periods are staggered into three groups.

Group One has an accounting date ending on 30 June, 30 September, 31 December and 31 March. Group Two has the accounting periods ending 31 July, 31 October, 31 January and 30 April. Group Three has accounting periods ending 31 August, 30 November, 28 February and 31 May. This is done to enable HM Customs and Excise to spread their work load so that they are not faced with every registered business sending in their returns at the same time.

If you commenced as a registered trader on, say, 2 May 1987 and you were allocated to Group Three for filing your VAT return, your first return would be up to the period ending 31 August 1987. After that date your VAT return would be submitted every three months.

However, in the case where you, as a taxable person, had consistently exceeded paying output tax and were due a repayment of VAT, it would adversely affect your cash flow as you would have to wait for anything up to three months for a return of any excess VAT already paid to HM Customs and Excise. In such situations it would be to your advantage to have a monthly tax period instead of a quarterly one. Therefore, it should be understood that the sequence of VAT returns does not necessarily coincide with the calendar quarters. The classification of your business dictates the stagger group into which you are allocated by HM Customs and Excise.

The VAT return itself summarises for any given tax period, the tax due and tax deductable either giving rise to a net figure of VAT payable to the Government's coffers or the amount repayable with regard to any excess inputs over outputs suffered by your business. This figure must also include any corrections (either against your tax situation or for it) arising from previous periods.

As mentioned earlier, your VAT account, maintained as part of your accounting records, will place you in a position to summarise easily your totals of output and input tax for each period. It is important that you should regularly add up the VAT figures in your accounting book and put the total of the VAT under the following separate headings.

Example:

VAT Deductible (Input Tax)	VAT Payable (Output Tax)
Purchases	Sales
Imports	Certain Postal Imports
	Imported Services
Errors in earlier returns	Errors in earlier returns
Any bad debt relief	

At the end of your allocated period you should add up the total under each of the seven headings (as already shown in your VAT account example on page 39) which will now place you in a position to complete Boxes 1 to 7 of the VAT return. The Return itself is known as VAT 100, and a copy of this is shown page 64.

The law requires that a registered person must submit this return no later than one calendar month after the end of the allocated period to the Southend computer centre. (A supply of envelopes should have been given to you by your local Customs and Excise office for this use.)

The VAT 100 form will automatically be sent to you a short time before the end of your allocated accounting date. Under no circumstances should a photocopy or an old form be used if you lose the form sent to you. Telephone your local VAT office and ask them to send you a replacement immediately.

The penalties for late submission of VAT returns are now punative and the days have long since gone where it was possible to obtain working capital for your business at the expense of VAT.

VAT default surcharges were introduced on 1 October 1986. Therefore any registered trader who submits the VAT return and pays the tax late on at least two occasions in any one year, will become liable to an automatic surcharge on the next occasion, within a 12 month period, for which his return is due. You will be liable to a default if your VAT return, and any part of the VAT arising in respect of that return, has not been received by the VAT central unit by the due date shown on your return. However, if you have defaulted twice in a 12 month period you will then be sent a surcharge liable notice. If you again default, having received that notice, in the following 12 months you will incur a surcharge which on the first occasion represents 5 per cent of the total amount of VAT payable by you. Once this default notice has been issued it will remain in force until you have submitted (as proof of good behaviour) all the VAT returns and accounted for all the VAT due by the due and payable dates in a 12 month period. This surcharge will increase by 5 per cent each time your VAT return and payment is late. Should you be late on a second occasion you will be charged not 5 per cent but 10 per cent. The third time will result in a surcharge of 15 per cent being levied against you. This will increase on each subsequent late payment up to a limit of 30 per cent of the VAT that is outstanding—a costly exercise indeed. (There is a minimal level of £30 below which no surcharge is levied.)

Although it is permissable to appeal against a surcharge liability, the only grounds you are likely to succeed on are if you can prove that your return and your VAT due and payable was despatched in time to arrive by the due date or give a reasonable excuse for the delay. Do note, however, that stressing lack of sufficient funds is not considered a reasonable excuse. Also bear in mind, that it is your responsibility to show that these returns have been lodged in time.

HM Customs and Excise do not consider it a reasonable excuse to say that you have instructed your accountant to have lodged and paid the respective tax within the time period. (Should this happen, although you will have to pay the amount due, you can, provided you take proper legal advice, take action against your accountant if it is his fault.) Incidentally, HM Customs and Excise hold a great deal of faith in the GPO's delivery system; should you be able to prove that you posted the envelope to them using a first class stamp the day before the due day, then the officer concerned will accept this delay. If you are going to play it this close to the wind, it is strongly recommended that you hold a certificate of posting, for example Special Delivery, Registered Post or Recorded Delivery. The latter is the cheapest form.

Therefore, to minimise your exposure to any penalty, it is important that you are not in default of any of your VAT periods. However, if due to an oversight you are in default for a VAT period, you must try not to default again in the following year. Should this happen and a notice is issued, you must take every available step to ensure that no further default takes place before the first anniversary of the VAT accounting period which first triggered the notice.

The same legislation introduced a repayment supplement in cases where the registered trader is owed a VAT *refund* by HM Customs and Excise and this has not been paid within a 30 day period. This refund situation can occur when your inputs exceed your outputs. To qualify for this repayment supplement all your VAT returns to date must have been submitted on time and the tax duly paid. The supplement itself is 5 per cent of tax overpaid or £30, whichever is the greatest.

VAT – A working guide for the small business

When completing your VAT 100 form you must not alter any of the details that are shown on the form that has been sent to you. For example, if your address has been noted incorrectly, you should notify your VAT office immediately but separately. There are a total of nine boxes to be completed on this form. Some of these boxes will probably not apply to you in which case you should write the word 'None'. See Figure 4 below.

Figure 4: Form VAT 100

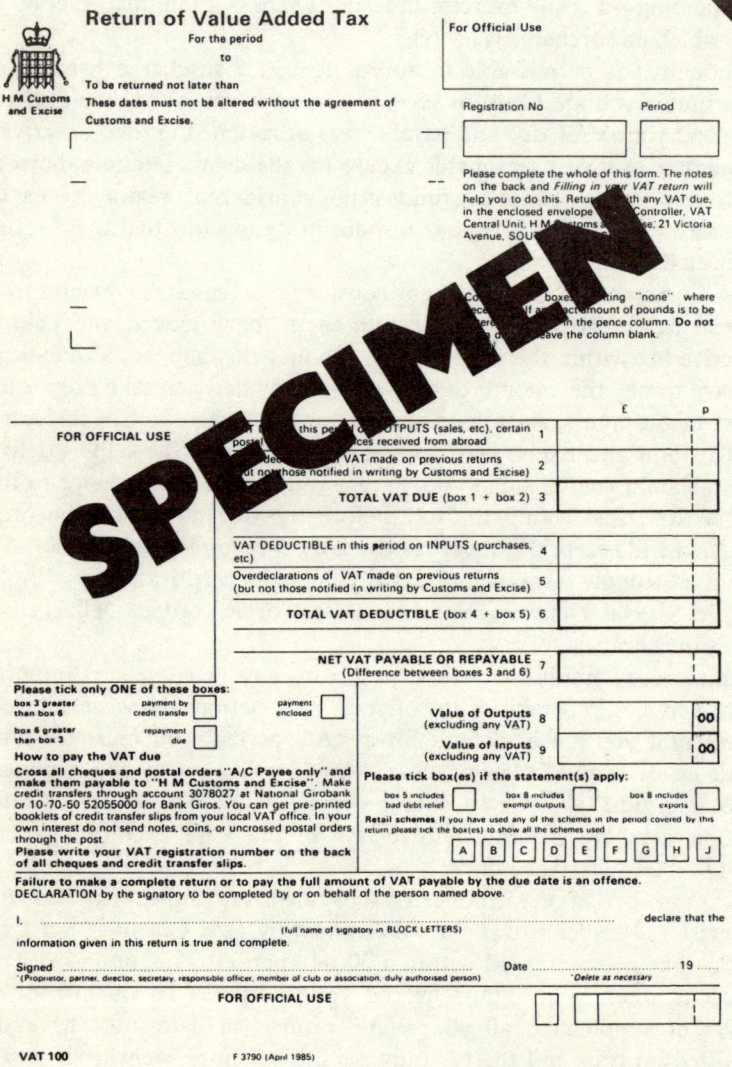

In Box 1, record the total amount of VAT due in respect of the VAT period. Basically, this is the VAT due on all your sales referred to as 'output tax'. This will include goods taken for private use, gifts or loan of goods, any sales made to staff and the sale of any business assets such as an office typewriter, desk and such like.

If, after completing your previous return, you discover that you have made a mistake in entering on your previous return too little VAT in Box 3 or you have overstated the amount of input tax on a previous return in Box 6, you can rectify this now by entering in Box 2, the difference owed by you.

In Box 3, you simply add up the totals of Box 1 and 2 to arrive at the total VAT due for this quarter.

In Box 4 you enter the VAT you have incurred on your purchases over the last three months. This is your input tax, see Chapter 5. But bear in mind, you cannot reclaim VAT on any purchases that have not been made in connection with your business i.e. entertaining, with the exception of overseas clients and motor cars.

In Box 5 you are given a chance to rectify mistakes made on earlier returns when you may have entered too much in Box 3 or claimed too little in Box 6. Therefore, you enter in Box 5 the difference that is owed to you by Customs and Excise. In addition, figures inserted in Box 5 can be used to claim back the VAT suffered on bad debts. This subject will be looked at in the next chapter.

Box 6 is simply the overall total of the total figures found in Boxes 4 and 5—rather like Box 3 but in reverse.

Box 7 is the culmination of the previous figures entered and will either result in a VAT liability or in a VAT repayment. You should take the figures in Boxes 3 and 6 and deduct the smaller amount from the larger amount and enter the resulting difference in Box 7.

If the figure in Box 3 is greater than that in Box 6 you will have a tax liability to pay to HM Customs and Excise. All cheques should be made payable to HM Customs and Excise and crossed 'account payee'.

By concession, a registered trader who has given an undertaking to discharge the VAT liability via the National Giro or the Giro system, as opposed to paying by cheque, is allowed an additional seven day period in which to pay his liability. You should note, however, that you have to obtain authority from Customs and Excise to do this.

The payment box shown towards the bottom of the VAT 100 form is the relevant box which needs to be ticked as either payment by 'credit transfer' or 'payment enclosed'.

If the figure you have entered in Box 3 is less than the figure entered in Box 6, you will be due for a refund and you should tick the 'repayment due' box.

In Box 8 you need to record the total amount of your quarterly sales *excluding VAT*. And in Box 9 you should enter the total amount of all the

VAT – A working guide for the small business

purchases you have made in the last three months, again leaving out the VAT charged for these items. From your point of view these two boxes may be superfluous, but these turnover figures help the Government's statistics in measuring the state of the economy.

Some items of income and expenditure have to be left out of Boxes 8 and 9, and it is up to you to choose between two systems known as 'Basis A' and 'Basis B'.

The latter is easier to administer than 'A' and as it has no direct relevance to your business, choose the Basis which is the easiest for you to work with.

Whichever you select you must continue to follow its conditions. In the case of selecting Basis A, you leave the following items out of Boxes 8 and 9:

(a) the VAT itself;
(b) all wages and salaries;
(c) all PAYE tax and NI contributions due on those salaries;
(d) all capital introduced or withdrawn from the business;
(e) any loan or payment of dividend, grant or gift of money;
(f) money received as a result of an insurance claim or compensation of a result of action brought by you;
(g) any profit or loss made through stock exchange dealings;
(h) those purchases which are outside the field of VAT defined as 'exempt', i.e. rent paid, bank charges, insurance premiums and bank interest;
(i) the road fund licence fee on your business vehicles together with the cost of an MOT certificate, if appropriate;
(j) the general rates and the water rates levied on your business, and finally;
(k) those purchases on which VAT cannot be reclaimed, such as VAT due on motor vehicles and entertaining UK clients.

If you decide to use Basis B you should leave out the items listed (a) to (g).

You now only need to print your full name and sign and date the return to complete it before sending it off to the Computer Centre in Southend.

If the circumstances relating to your business alter, you must write to your local VAT office as soon as possible giving full details. Do not wait until the next VAT return is due. You may find that if the VAT return is not sent in on time, a reminder may be received. If you persistently do not submit the return, Customs and Excise could well send you an estimate (form VAT 151) which is more than likely to be excessive. You must lodge an appeal against this immediately.

Should you find that you cannot pay all your VAT at once, do not delay in sending in your VAT 100 form. It is also worth noting that you should not send in post dated cheques as these are unlikely to be accepted by

VAT returns

HM Customs and Excise. Instead, write to your local VAT office as soon as possible explaining the reasons why you cannot pay. More than likely you will be able to reach an agreement whereby you pay the outstanding liability over a short period of time. In Chapter 11 we will look at ways of dealing with HM Customs and Excise.

VAT payable on the discounted price regardless of whether the customer takes advantage of the offer or not.

Disposal of assets

As the transfer or disposal of assets used in the course of your business is a supply of goods, even if no money is received, it is important to recognise that the scrapping of machinery may constitute a supply of goods and give rise to a potential VAT liability. An example of this would be where factory equipment is removed by a scrap metal merchant.

Partial exemption

During the course of running your business it is more than likely that you will be making a range of different supplies, some of which may be exempt supplies, some of which will carry the full rate of VAT at 15 per cent and others which will be zero rated. If you were making only exempt supplies, as we have seen earlier, you would not be making any taxable supplies and so would not be eligible to register for VAT purposes and reclaim any of your input tax. How much tax, therefore, can someone claim back when making a mixture of supplies?

In the simplest of situations, referred to here as Standard Method A, you would have to measure the approximate proportions of exempt and taxable supplies. This would enable you to reclaim input tax in the same proportion as that which the taxable supplies bear to the total supplies.

In Standard Method B, the law recognises that a trader who is partly exempt will acquire goods which are sold on in exactly the same state as that in which they were bought. Here we are thinking of banks who in the past have become involved in leasing transactions, for tax purposes. Under Standard Method B such leasing transactions are separated from the rest of the partial exempt calculations, so that the full input tax can be offset against output tax without suffering any restriction.

Since either of these methods can produce a tax liability situation which is acceptable to neither Customs and Excise or the trader, it is up to the individual to devise a 'customised' method which is acceptable to Customs and Excise and which produces a fairer result. The most common of these special methods is known as the 'Directly Attributable' method, whereby each business activity is examined and input tax attributed to each particular field. No doubt certain overhead expenditure will remain where direct attribution is not possible and here Standard Method A could be used.

Because of these various complications, the following *de-minimis* limits have been introduced to enable a taxable person to avoid any restriction and loss of input tax if the value of exempt supplies in any VAT quarter does not exceed:

(1) £200 per month on average, or

(2) both £8000 per month on average and 50 per cent of the value of all supplies made, or

(3) both £16000 per month on average and 25 per cent of the value of all supplies, or

(4) one per cent of the value of all supplies made.

Further *de-minimis* relief will apply in respect of input tax but can only be used when the Direct Attribution method has been adopted if exempt supplies are both less than 5 per cent of total input tax and, on average, £200 or less. Meeting these requirements allows your business to be regarded as fully taxable and enables reclamation of all input tax suffered. The main objective of these *de-minimis* limits is to save on administrative costs in collecting small amounts of VAT.

These partial exemption calculations are made on a quarterly basis and seasonal fluctuations in trade may lead to inequitable results. For this reason you have to carry out an annual adjustment at the end of your VAT year—March, April or May depending on your stagger-grouping. This exercise will involve the recalculation of the mix of exempt and taxable outputs over the last twelve months, with the new percentage being applied to the total of input tax suffered in the same period. The net result will be either the need for a further payment to HM Customs and Excise or a claim for a refund from them.

As previously stated, a group of companies can seek group registration. This enables all the supplies made by and to members of such a group to be treated as having been made by or to the representative member. Thus a company with a small level of exempt outputs would be able to group itself with another company, under common control, which may have substantial taxable outputs. By combining the two, however, they could well fall within the 5 per cent *de-minimis* limits. Similar advantages could also be achieved in respect of the 'Input Rules' already defined.

A partly exempt person must exclude from his partial exemption calculations the exempt outputs that have been generated by

(1) capital sums that have been received by the exempt supply arising from the grant, assignment or surrender of an interest in land, including any building which has been habitually occupied during the course of carrying on a trade, and

(2) the receipt of interest, unless it is in the main part of your business to receive such money (for example, a solicitor would not become partly exempt just because he receives money held on clients' accounts).

Partial exemption can also give rise to unexpected additional tax liabilities, such as in the case of a person registered for VAT purposes who may import certain specified services. He would then have to account for the output tax as if he had made the supply himself and at the same time

Particular situations relating to your business

be able to reclaim all his input tax. However, if that person were partially exempt, the input tax would be restricted but the output tax would remain payable in full. This would, for example, apply to a UK based insurance company settling an overseas claim.

10 VAT Planning

Unlike income tax planning, VAT does not necessitate complicated schemes involving the insertion of a series of artificial transactions in an attempt to make large amounts of tax liabilities disappear. Instead, it involves avoiding the creation of an unnecessary tax liability in the first place, as once a supply has been made it is impossible to reverse the situation and remove the VAT due on the supply. VAT planning centres more on meticulous attention to detail and timing than on anything else. As an example, a builder who may have been engaged in the construction of new buildings could reduce his VAT loss if, when he decided to extend his business activities into the field of refurbishment, he so timed his operations that any supplies made to him were made over one extended period with supplies connected with the refurbished building being made in the subsequent period.

A number of ways exist whereby the amount of input tax that may be claimed can be improved. For example, someone who is constructing a building and is obliged to sell it by way of an exempt lease, i.e. 21 years or less. The builder in this case should first sell the building to an associated company in order to establish a zero rated supply and hence the right to receive all the relevant input tax. The associated company should be one that has been specially set up for the purpose so that it has little or no input tax whose recovery would be restricted by the effects of the exempt supply of the lease.

The reason why you should be paying particular attention to VAT planning in the first instance is obvious – if you do not, large sums of money will be lost. This will either reduce the level of your profits or can even increase a loss that you have already made. One of the major reasons for planning your affairs is because of the time lag between introducing a wrong method of accounting for VAT and finding out afterwards it is wrong – it is one of the greatest 'loss' makers too! For example, an operation undertaken by you today which gives rise to excess VAT liability may not come to light until Customs and Excise visit you in, say, 1990. At that late stage an assessment may well be raised on your trading activities in a direct tax accounting period which is, in actual fact, long since finalised.

It is as well to remember that because of the continuing nature of VAT and the fact that the tax is payable on turnover, a very large liability can quickly accrue. Under the 1985 Finance Act, there are very stringent penalties which can be levied on the unwary or those who have not been sufficiently prudent in their accounting procedures. As examples a number of recent cases spring to mind ranging from a model who had not realised her fees took her over the VAT limits, to a well known horse trainer whose case is still under investigation.

Conversely, if you do not fully understand the nature of the supplies made by you this may well result in too much VAT being paid to Customs and Excise. Sadly, this tax could well be irrecoverable, which in turn could obviously reduce profitability.

The optimum situation for any business as far as VAT is concerned is for it to be making only zero rated supplies which will enable it to reclaim all of the tax paid on the supplies being made and at the same time not to having to charge VAT to its own customers. Conversely, the worst position for any business is to find itself not registered for VAT and therefore unable to claim any of the tax back. This business will suffer financially in that supplies invoiced to it will have VAT included, whilst it will have to absorb these amounts instead of setting them against VAT output charged to its clients. Thus, the overheads of this business will suffer as the value will show an inflated amount – inflated by the VAT already paid.

The majority of VAT planning will undoubtedly centre around large groups of companies and group elections, which clearly fall outside the scope of this book. However, having said that, good accounting practices are still essential whatever the size of the business, and the timing of invoices can be used to affect the cash flow position of any business, provided it is not operating under the new cash accounting method for VAT.

Specific areas for attention

Whenever possible, any capital expenditure made by you, in the course of running your business, should be made at the end of your accounting period for VAT so that the amount reclaimed as input tax will coincide with the payment you have had to make to the supplier. Also, whenever possible, any particularly large invoices should be raised right at the beginning of the VAT quarter, just in case your customers are late in paying you. Even if they do pay you, you will have the use of the Government's money for a longer period of time before having to 'pay it across' and this will no doubt assist your cash flow.

If you are in the service industries, such as design consultant, and your 'supply' of services is on a continuing basis of trade (which could involve a number of months in excess of your VAT quarter) and the issue of your tax invoice is the form of a fee notice, then should your client not pay before the tax is due to Customs and Excise you will have to account for the liability out of your own pocket. This situation is a negative one for a small trader and can have serious consequences on your ability to continue trading – especially if your client base is small, i.e. four or less clients. This situation can easily be avoided by the issue of a proforma invoice. However, do tell your customer that your business is conducted in this way before sending off the invoice. This proforma invoice should clearly state that it is not a VAT invoice and so will not include details of your VAT registration number. The total amount, however, should be the same as for the VAT invoice, but VAT would not be shown as a separate item, i.e. 'in settlement of "X": total £115'. When your client does actually settle the account, the date of payment crystallises the tax point. The invoice which now has to be raised shows the VAT registration number and the breakdown of 'in settlement of "X" £100; VAT £15; total due £115'.

Within 30 days of receiving the money you must forward to your client a proper VAT invoice. Ignoring the provisions of the new cash accounting system, this procedure ensures that no VAT is payable until payment is received.

One area where the small businessman has far more scope for VAT planning than the large company is in the choice of whether he should register for VAT in the first place or whether in fact – if the turnover is below the limits – it would be more beneficial to de-register.

If your taxable turnover is below the registration threshold – currently £21,300 per annum – you might well decide that it is simpler not to increase the level of your turnover, so removing the necessity to register for VAT. In some businesses which are directly consumer related, such as a painter or a decorator, registering could have an adverse effect on trade, as it would necessitate adding VAT on to prices and thus increase the amount to be paid by your clients who in most cases will not be VAT registered. Should this apply to you and if your turnover was just above the registration threshold of £21,300, it might well pay you to reduce the level of your turnover to below the limits of voluntary de-registration – currently £20,500 per annum – in order to compete with other painters and decorators on price.

As being registered for VAT has hidden costs in the form of your own time and effort spent in keeping these additional records, a business that makes zero rated supplies can request voluntary exemption from registration under paragraph 11(1) of Schedule 1 of the Value Added Tax Act 1983. Some businesses, however, feel that to be registered will improve their market image, and this is particularly true for new companies who feel that they will lose credibility when dealing with large customers.

These companies often registered for VAT despite the fact that their turnover is well below the threshsold set. Before you contemplate registering for this reason there are two points which you should bear in mind. Firstly, you will have to show HM Customs and Excise that there is a 'compelling business need' for you to be registered. Secondly, remember that there will be time lost spent in sitting through the control visits made by Customs and Excise and for the uninitiated this can be quite a traumatic experience.

Although VAT is supposed to be a neutral tax on businesses, in actual fact it can and does effect your profits. To calculate the impact of registration or de-registration, you need to calculate your net profit on the basis that no input tax can be reclaimed (if you were registered) and there is no need to account for output tax on your bought in supplies. Then you should calculate your net profit on the basis that all input tax can be reclaimed and output tax at ⅔rds of your total turnover must be paid. Now compare the two figures. Whichever of the two shows the greatest profit for your business should be the one you choose.

Having decided that either you should register for VAT or you will have to register for VAT, the timing of registration, as far as VAT planning is concerned, is important. By careful selection you can delay or accelerate your VAT registration by postponing or bringing forward your tax point.

Finally, a well tried and tested method of avoiding registration (and one acceptable to HM Customs and Excise) is to split your various business interests into totally separate entities. You will no doubt recall that it is the person who is registered for VAT and not the business. For example, if you run a local cornershop and are registered for VAT purposes and you also offer bed and breakfast accommodation, you must account for VAT on this activity too. If however, your wife ran the bed and breakfast side and provided her turnover did not exceed £21,300, there would be no requirement for her to register for VAT. It is the taxable turnover of each person which creates the liability, not the aggregate of the two individuals, even though they are connected through marriage. Taking the husband and wife situation a stage further, it is possible to create a third person for VAT registration purposes, i.e. the husband is sole proprietor of one business, he is in partnership with his wife in another and his wife is the sole proprietor of the third business.

A further fairly common example is the local village pub owned jointly by a husband and wife. The pub not only sells drinks but also pub lunches and offers a service of overnight accommodation. There is nothing to stop the pub being operated by the wife as sole proprietor and the bed and breakfast side of the business being operated as a separate entity by the husband – as sole trader, of course.

This method of 'business splitting', as it is known, will, of course, only be worthwhile if the saving of output tax exceeds any loss of input tax. You should remember here that the input tax attributable to the non-registered portion of your business is non-recoverable and any attempt to route such input tax through the registered portion of your business will be clocked by HM Customs and Excise on one of their visits. If you did this you would be breaking VAT regulations, which is strongly advised against and could well leave you open to a penalty.

It has been stated by HM Customs and Excise, in their press release of 20 September 1982, that for existing businesses to be split for VAT registration purposes certain conditions must be met. These are:

(1) The appropriate premises and equipment are owned or rented by the person carrying on the business.

(2) Separate accounts for each new part of the business are maintained.

(3) Purchase and sales invoices should be in the name of the person carrying on each part of the business.

(4) The person who is carrying on the said business should be the one who is legally responsible for paying suppliers, etc. and should be the one entitled to the rewards from the trade.

(5) The business's bank account should be in that person's name and that person alone should be able to make withdrawals from it.

(6) All wages and National Insurance contributions should remain the responsibility of the person who is carrying on the business in respect of all members of staff employed in that part of the trade.

(7) A separate income tax assessment should be raised in respect of the part of the business that has been hived off.

The areas discussed in this chapter clearly show the need for prior planning and – as has already been noted – once the supply has been made then it is too late to implement VAT planning. Consideration as to when to register and when to invoice (and how) are very important, and, of course, there is the possibility of 'business splitting'. But on no account should you break VAT regulations. Remember, HM Customs and Excise has very stringent powers indeed!

11 Dealing with HM Customs and Excise

The Department of HM Customs and Excise has enormous powers in all matters relating to the collection and operation of indirection taxation. Powers far in excess of those granted for example, to the police or indeed the Inland Revenue. It can be seen that some of the measures introduced, a few examples are noted below, are heavily biased against the trader since in some cases the trader not only has to watch out for his own errors but those made by HM Customs and Excise too.

The latest power awarded to Customs and Excise is the implementation of many of the recommendations of the Keith Committee, now in the form of the 1985 Finance Act, already referred to in several places throughout this book. Under this Act, a civil offence known as 'Tax Evasion: Conduct involving dishonest conduct' has been created.

To date, there are approximately 5,000 business people—mainly new businesses—who have been discovered under the late registration regulations first introduced in July 1985. These people have now rendered themselves liable to penalties running into thousands of pounds and even imprisonment at Her Majesty's pleasure.

The importance of timely registration has constantly been stressed and here again it must be stated that once you *are aware* that the current level of £21,300 *will be exceeded* you must apply for registration. The words here have been deliberately emphasised as it is not the same to become aware, for example, when your annual historic accounts have been prepared. This means, therefore, that there is a requirement on your part to monitor your quarterly turnover so that you can reasonably know whether or not your future turnover will exceed that set limit. Any accountant worth his salt will also remind you—on a constant basis, hopefully—that this level must be watched. HM Customs and Excise has taken the view (which has been supported in the Courts) that the date of registration must be taken from the date that you *should have been aware* of the requirement to register. Failure to do so carries a mandatory penalty of 30 per cent of the VAT due in cases where the need for late registration has been proved. This applies even if all the tax could have been claimed as input tax and all the output tax would have subsequently been reclaimed by your customers as their input tax. This is done so that there will be no loss to the Crown.

It is useful at this point to cite an example. A girl who was only 19 years of age started her first job as a model in April 1985 and soon began earning large sums of money. It was not until the 12 March 1986 that she registered for VAT but Customs and Excise said that she should have registered on the 21 October 1985 and demanded a penalty of £212 for being late. The model appealed to the VAT tribunal claiming she had a 'reasonable excuse' for being late. The 'reasonable excuse' given was that she had no way of knowing she should have been registered for VAT because of the unusual way in which she was paid; payments were based on vouchers given to her by her agency. The agency then prepared invoices from these vouchers but until a model was VAT registered it was not their policy to supply her with copy invoices. However, the VAT tribunal refused to accept the argument and the fine was duly confirmed.

It used to be the case that failure to receive acknowledgement of your application to register for VAT from HM Customs and Excise, even if it was sent in due time, was held to be a reasonable excuse. This is no longer the case following another VAT tribunal's ruling. This ruling has blocked the loophole of business's claiming that they had sent in their registration forms, when in fact they had not. Therefore not only should you monitor your turnover watching out for the threshold limits but now, once you are aware that those limits will be exceeded and you send in your registration form, if you do not hear from the Registration Unit within 21 days, *you* must follow it up. Liability for any oversight at the Department or delay en route has now been passed on to you.

Other statutory penalties are contained in Section 14 of the 1985 Finance Act relating to 'Serious misdeclaration or neglect resulting in understatements or overclaims'. Failure to observe these rules will render you liable to a penalty of 30 per cent of the lost tax. This rule also covers cases where as a result of no return being made, an estimated assessment has been issued in its place but is too low and you fail to draw this to the attention of the Commissioners within a 30 day period. The penalty only becomes chargeable if these underdeclarations or overstatements equal or exceed 30 per cent of the true amount of VAT payable.

As has been seen earlier in this book, if you delay sending in your VAT return form (VAT 100) on two occasions over a twelve month period, you will be served a surcharge liability notice. If you are again late in sending in your return you will have incurred an automatic penalty of five per cent of the VAT owed, subject to a minimum of £30 and this will, on subsequent occasions of late returns, be increased up to a ceiling of 30 per cent of the tax due. It is most important therefore that you understand how VAT affects your business so that you can avoid these pitfalls.

The Taxpayers Charter

In July 1986, HM Customs and Excise published what is known as their 'Taxpayers Charter'. This document explains how Customs and Excise see *their responsibilities towards you*. This can be summarised as follows.

Help and information: the staff of Customs and Excise are there to help you in every reasonable way to obtain your legal rights so that you can meet your obligations under the existing tax laws. They can only do this if you give them the full facts that they need to decide upon how much tax is due from you.

Courtesy and consideration: the staff of Customs and Excise should at all times carry out their duties courteously, considerately and promptly. [Afterall, we do pay their wages and without us they would be without a job.]

Fairness: you have the right to expect that your VAT liability will be decided impartially, that you will not be asked to pay more than your true liability and that you should not be asked for more than anyone else in similar circumstances. Customs and Excise will assume that you are honest unless they have reason to believe that you are not.

Privacy and confidentiality: any information that you give to HM Customs and Excise will be treated in strict confidence.

Costs of compliance: in asking you to comply with the law they will endeavour to keep your costs to a minimum.

Independent appeal and review: the Collector of Customs and Excise will always look again at your case and if you are still not satisfied you may appeal against a VAT decision to the independent VAT tribunal. [Failing that there is nothing quite like getting a Government department moving than to ask your Member of Parliament to take the matter up on your behalf or ask the Ombudsman to look at your case again.]

The extent of HM Customs and Excise's powers

Customs and Excise's authority is such that they will request all accounting records and files—including confidential correspondence—which you will be obliged to give. The usual practice on these visits is to inspect your invoice files first. As all accounting documentation will be asked for, it is appropriate to reiterate the importance of keeping all accounting records up to date and in good order.

A search cannot, of course, be made of your premises without a search warrant being applied for, although samples of your goods may be taken away. A receipt must also be given. Customs and Excise have the power to arrest you without a warrant, but may only exercise this power in cases of serious offences.

Needless to say, should matters be serious enough for this action to be thought necessary, then proper legal advice and representation must be sought.

A visit from the VAT-man

As a VAT registered business you will receive a control visit from HM Customs and Excise on average once every four years. This is because it is the duty of the VAT office to check that your business is complying with the tax regulations and satisfying themselves that the VAT returns and the tax payments reflected in those returns are indeed true. Over the years, 85 per cent of all returns were submitted late and at any one time some £1 billion of VAT has been outstanding to the Government.

When you have registered you must prepare yourself for regular visits from HM Customs and Excise. These visits are made to check that declarations are in order and can vary in length from under one hour to a week or more. Prior notice is usually given, although they have the right of entry at any reasonable time. If the arranged time is inconvenient as you have, say, booked to go away to Portugal on holiday at the start of that week, you would not be expected to cancel your holiday, but naturally you would have to make a mutually convenient appointment for as soon as possible after your return.

When the VAT officer visits you, he is most likely to have come from the Central Directorate and in most cases has had little experience in actually running a business. You may find therefore that he does not appreciate how you run and operate your business, so make sure you explain to him in the clearest possible language how everything relating to your business operates.

Never forget that during VAT inspections the officer will be taking down notes, so avoid making incautious and uninformed remarks as they could well cost you dear at a later date.

If asked a specific question during the visit it is much safer to reply that 'you believe this or that to be the case but that you will have to check the position'. Never, but never, assume that the VAT officer knows what you are talking about. Whilst they have basic bookkeeping knowledge they are *not* accountants.

If you are not sure whether you should be charging VAT on a particular invoice do not wait until you have a control visit, because if you have not charged VAT when you should have done so then an assessment will be raised and in addition you may be liable for a penalty. If, however, you have previously advised the Customs office of a possible underdeclaration, although you will still be responsible for the tax, you will not have rendered yourself liable for a penalty.

Dealing with HM Customs and Excise

During the routine visit you may wish to clarify certain points with the control officer. In such circumstances it is always advisable, when asking about your VAT liability, to ask for written confirmation concerning the information requested given that the statements made by the VAT officer may well only be his opinion and not that of the Department. As such they could well be misinterpreted.

Control visits usually last for a few hours (although should errors be found this can be extended into days and weeks, calling in the business's firm of accountants to help sort matters out). Hopefully, and in your best interest, your records will be up to date and your filing system tidy – it never hurts to create a good impression. Whilst you should co-operate with the VAT officer remember that he is there to collect the maximum amount of tax from your business and will, no doubt, be asking questions about it, what controls you operate and what cash sales are made. This latter area is one where tax liability may not be fully recorded, hence the interest shown.

All the trading accounts will be examined by the officer to reconcile the sales figures shown in your financial accounts with those shown on the VAT return. He will pay particular attention to the non-deductible input tax items, such as business entertainment.

During the course of the officer's visit, notes will be taken in case of future disputes. As it is one man's word against another and as these officers usually travel in pairs, it is essential that you take your own notes as written proof – from your side of things – of the conversation and resultant implications. Indeed, it is good advice to have a witness present especially if the discussion concerns a follow-up visit.

If, following a VAT inspector's visit, Customs and Excise alleges a VAT error, always request that this be stated in writing specifying the nature of the default. Upon receipt, reply to the VAT office concerned acknowledging receipt of their letter. It is advisable at this stage to consult with a tax specialist.

Sometimes an error will be found in your favour, as in the case of underdeclarations of input tax, but in most cases they will be asking you to pay more tax and as such will raise an assessment. If you do not agree with the VAT man's findings, you have the option of appealing to a VAT tribunal and if this goes against you there is always the High Court. Remember, however, that should the action go against you at that stage, the costs incurred could well bankrupt you, not to mention the mental stress put on you and your family. However, in most cases agreement can be reached prior to the case coming before the tribunal. Do ensure that any agreement reached is put in writing. If you subsequently wish to withdraw from this agreement you have only 30 days to do so.

As mentioned before, if you do not submit a VAT return an estimated assessment will follow. If this assessment is not paid or an appeal lodged against it, then interest will be charged from the date the tax should have been paid until the day it is actually paid. If the assessment turns out to be too low, the difference is still payable and if it is in relation to an overdue return, then a penalty will also be added. Although records should be retained for six years it may be advisable to keep them for a longer period, just in case something comes to light as a result of a control visit at a later date. Remember also that if you are proposing a course of action and are unclear as to the VAT consequences, it is always possible to obtain advance clearance from HM Customs and Excise on a 'no names' basis. However, in such cases, all material facts should be laid before them as otherwise the ruling given will be withdrawn.

Finally, in order to make the matters crystal clear, remember that Customs and Excise tend to try to enforce the law *as they see it*. Because of this, it is often up to individuals to fight the matter out by taking their case to the European Court of Justice in Luxembourg. This is currently happening with several British companies who use sales promotions techniques whereby gifts bought at a discounted price are given away to party hostesses. These items are currenty attracting VAT at the normal retail price. Customs and Excise argues that the companies are enjoying the value of the house party and so this is an 'assumed consideration'. However, the concept of 'assumed consideration' does not in actual fact apply in European law (where, you will recall, VAT originated). If the appeal is successful then HM Customs and Excise will be forced to change their ways and the companies themselves will have won a large rebate. The lesson to be learned, if the European Court finds in favour of the companies involved, is never to be afraid to take matters to the highest level provided you are clearly and proveable in the right. Do not take for granted that because Customs and Excise is an official Government body it is right. This is not always the case.

12 De-registration

In our final chapter it is important that the subject of de-registration be turned to. You may have been one of those businesses to have decided early on in its formation that – irrespective of turnover – VAT registration was necessary. On the other hand, you may at some stage in the past have had to register for VAT but now find that your turnover has fallen below the VAT trading threshold. HM Customs and Excise may be called many things but one thing they cannot be called is unfair, particularly when relating to this uncommon problem. De-registration is therefore permitted provided certain criteria can be established. These will be looked at later in the chapter, but firstly the problem of an unexpected tax liability must be dealt with.

De-registration may produce an unexpected liability to tax on the deemed supply of business assets, such as office equipment, as well as all your manufactured goods held in stock at the time of de-registration, unless the VAT that would be due and payable does not exceed £250. And this amount, as you can see, is a small sum indeed.

Remember when dealing with VAT that the level of VAT threshold both for registration and de-registration normally adjusts itself upwards each financial year. Usually this adjustment is based on the annual percentage rate (a growth/inflation rate used by Government as a common yardstick when evaluating just such areas).

Applying for de-registration

You may voluntarily apply for de-registration if after the end of any calendar quarter the value of your taxable supplies in each of the last two years has been £20,500 or less (current level) and that you have been registered for VAT during the whole of those two years. Also, you must have no reason to believe that the value of all your taxable supplies in the following twelve months will exceed £20,500. If this criteria can be met then your VAT registration will be cancelled 14 days from the date you notified HM Customs and Excise.

A VAT registered business can also de-register at any time if it can satisfy Customs and Excise that the vaue of future taxable supplies for a period of one year will not exceed £19,500. Again, registration would be cancelled. It is also allowable by Customs and Excise for a VAT registered trader, who has only registered under the Voluntary Registration provisions, to withdraw his request for registration. So far it has all appeared to be rather simple, but it is worth remembering that Customs and Excise can refuse your request if you have not been registered for a period of two years. Thus, it is important to bear this in mind when first applying to be voluntarily registered. Again, we can take the example of the business whose proprietors feel that it is justifiable for business/marketing status to be registered.

Progressing this example further, suppose the business misled Customs and Excise into granting registration based on an expected turnover. Further suppose that this turnover has not been reached. VAT registration would automatically be cancelled from day one *unless* they could show that they had reasonable grounds for believing that the business would have attained a turnover of at least £21,300 over a twelve month period.

Another area to which attention should be paid is compulsory de-registration. If you were intending to trade and voluntarily registered for VAT but did not in fact make any taxable supplies by the date you stated, then Customs and Excise could compulsorily force you into de-registration. It is most important therefore that you make the supplies you said you would when you said you would, as Customs and Excise has the power to claw back all the input tax that you have claimed. An expensive error indeed!

There is yet another circumstance to bear in mind which gives rise to de-registration. In cases where a VAT registered trader's taxable turnover has dropped to below the level where he could voluntarily de-registered but he has not done so and has also failed to lodge a VAT return with HM Customs and Excise, then the authority has the power to withdraw the registration. Those persons who carry voluntary registration will also lose that right if it appears to Customs and Excise that they should no longer be registered. Having said all this, it must not be forgotten that you have the right to appeal against the decision by taking your case to a VAT tribunal. However, it is most important that all dealings have been carried out according to the rules and regulations governing the operation of VAT.

Certain other changes to your business will also trigger off the cancellation of your registration. For example, if you decide to turn your sole trader status into that of a limit company, upon de-registration VAT will be accounted for on the final VAT return in respect of all the goods that form part of your business at the close of trade, or on the last day of registration.

De-registration

When you close down you business or sell it on, you must de-register. It is not always clear at what point you are seen to have 'ceased' trading in this business. As a guide, it would be safe to assume that you have in fact ceased trading when you have made your final sale. It is compulsory to notify HM Customs and Excise within the allowable 30 days after the date of sale. Failure to do so can incur a penalty of £10 per day for each day until you notify the authority.

A point of interest here; there is no deemed supply if the business was transferred as a going concern to another person who is or will become registered, when you die or become bankrupt.

As previously stated, but worthy of a reminder, output tax will become chargeable on all your business assets on which you have previously claimed input tax – at time of purchase, say – unless the value of those assets is below £1,666 and the minimum VAT applicable is only £250 (£1,666 at 15 per cent).

This is where an element of VAT planning is useful with regard to timing. Before de-registering, assets should be sold on and de-registration should not take place until these assets have actually been sold thereby forming part of the output tax. This is passed on to the purchaser who, if VAT registered, can claim it as an input. In circumstances where de-registration must take place before the goods can actually be sold, issue an invoice to your purchaser prior to the de-registration. In this instance it is based on the invoiced amount for the goods and not on the supply of them.

When you de-register it stands to reason that you cannot issue tax invoices. Before cancellation make sure that invoices have been issued in respect of all goods and services supplied by you. Naturally, no input tax should be reclaimed after you have de-registered. Special arrangements do exist to cover invoices for services that are awaited but as yet have not been included in the final return, for example, your accountant's bill for completing your final accounts. As a rough guide, the claim for any such items should be made within a six month period after de-registration.

Once your registration has been cancelled you will be sent a final VAT Return form (193), as shown on page 94. This form covers the period of time from the end of your last VAT quarter to the date of cancellation. Information put on all forms is well-worth a double check, and this final form should be no exception.

VAT – A working guide for the small business

Figure 6: Form VAT 193

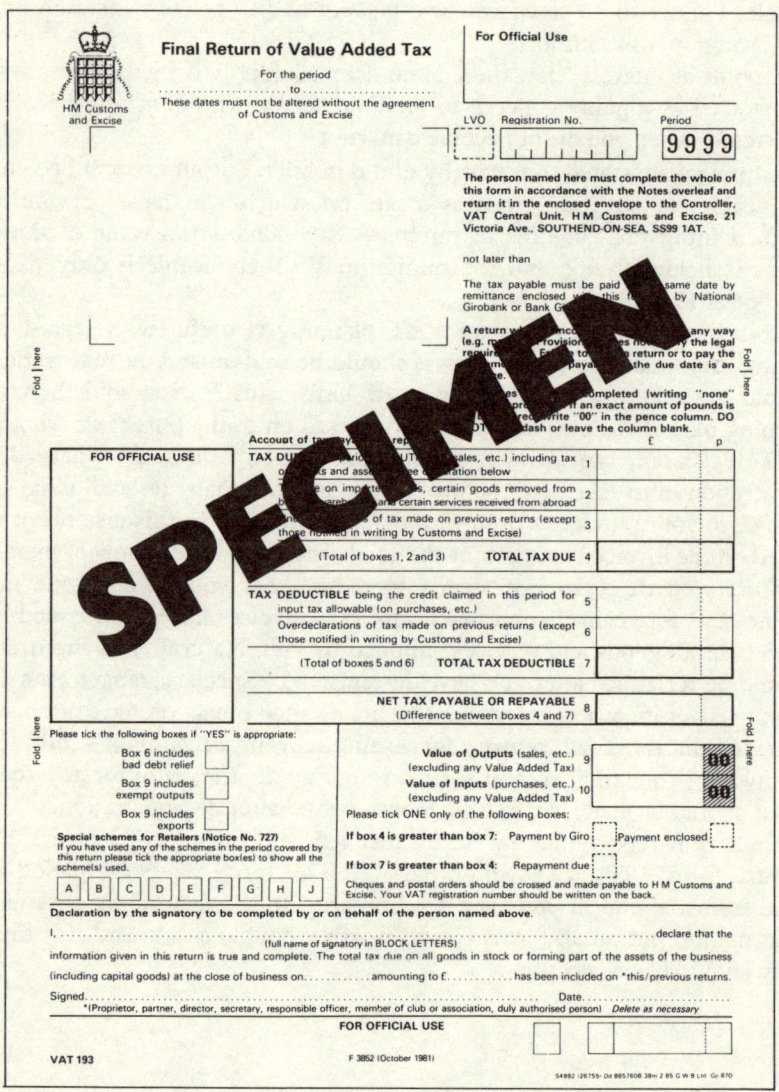

Conclusion

Without doubt, VAT does mean extra work for you and if you are a sole trader – which many readers will be – this must be taken into consideration.

This book has dealt with the subject of VAT in the sequence in which it will normally apply, hence VAT planning and de-registration are at the end. The book started off stating – truly – that VAT is a complex subject little understood and therefore often ignored to the detriment of traders. Hopefully, after reading this book, you are in a better position to handle your VAT affairs and use the system to your advantage in the course of your business.

APPENDIX I

VAT Offices

Please note that sub-offices are not included in the list below, because they do not normally deal with general enquiries.

Boundaries are subject to change from time to time, so it is wise to telephone the selected office before writing or calling, to ensure that it is indeed the one responsible for the business concerned.

Aberdeen Athol Ho. 84-88 Guild St Aberdeen AB9 2DY: 0224 574567
Accrington Oakbank Ho. Oak St Accrington BB5 1JD: 0254 31101
Alperton Crown Ho. North Circular Rd London NW10 7SU: 01-965 8700

Bath Ham Gardens Ho. Ham Gardens Bath BA1 1HR: 0225 65931
Bedford Graylaw Ho. 21/21A Goldington Rd Bedford MK40 3NL: 0234 63266
Belfast PO Box 21 Custom Ho. Belfast BT1 3EU: 0232 234466
Birmingham 2 Broadway Broad St Birmingham B15 1BG: 021-643 2233
Bootle Heron Ho. Hougomont Ave Crosby Liverpool L22 0PY: 051-920 4255
Bradford 87 Manningham Lane Bradford BD1 3DD: 0274 734581
Brighton Old Cottage South Rd Preston Village Brighton BN1 6TA: 0273 507244
Bristol Froomsgate Ho. Rupert St Bristol BS1 2QP: 0272 266091
Bury Derby Ho. Derby St Bury BL9 0NR: 061-761 4511

VAT – A working guide for the small business

Canterbury Park Ho. Sturry Rd
Canterbury CT1 1DJ: 0227 69461
Cardiff Portcullis Ho. 21 Cowbridge
Rd East Cardiff CF1 9SS:
0222 388531
Carlisle Hilltop Heights London Rd
Harraby Carlisle CA1 2NR:
0228 31222
Carmarthen Lyric Bldgs 6 King St
Carmarthen SA31 1BT: 0267 234111
Cheadle 2B Carrs Rd Cheadle
SK8 2HW: 061-428 3611
Chester Centurion Ho. 77 Northgate
St Chester CH1 2JZ: 0244 31555
Chesterfield St Marys Gate
Chesterfield S41 7TJ: 0246 204881
City 30 Finsbury Sq London
EC2A 1TD: 01-628 4232
Colchester Portal Ho. 27 Southway
Colchester CO3 3ER: 0206 563154
Coleraine Mill Ho. 24 Railway Rd
Coleraine Co Londonderry
BT52 1PH: 0265 4803/4 and 51684
Colwyn Bay Govt. Bldgs. Dinerth
Rd Colwyn Bay Clwyd LL29 4UL:
0492 44261
Coventry Hertford Ho. Hertford St
Coventry CV1 1PL: 0203 555111
Croydon AMP Ho. Dingwall Rd
Croydon CR9 3RQ: 01-680 1700

Derby Gower Ho. Gower St Derby
DE1 1NQ: 0332 362121
Doncaster Weston Ho. 92/98
Cleveland St Doncaster DN1 3LG:
0302 68641
Douglas Customs & Excise Isle of
Man Govt. VAT Office Custom Ho.
North Quay Douglas Isle of Man
0624 74321
Droitwich Government Bldgs
Worcester Droitwich WR9 8BT:
0905 774111
Dudley Trident Ho. 14
Wolverhampton St Dudley
DY1 1QL: 0384 56980

Edinburgh North 44 York Place
Edinburgh EH1 3JW: 031-556 2433
Edinburgh South As for Edinburgh
North

Local VAT offices listing

Enfield Burleigh Ho. 101/143 Gt Cambridge Rd Enfield EN1 1UH: 01-366 6666
Exeter Renslade Ho. Bonhay Rd Exeter EX4 3DA: 0392 79081

Finchley Anneuel Ho. 707 High Rd Finchley London N12 0BW: 01-446 1400

Glasgow North Portcullis Ho. 21 India St Glasgow G2 4PZ: 041-221 3828
Glasgow South As for Glasgow North
Gloucester Elmbridge Court Cheltenham Rd Gloucester GL3 1JX: 0452 36522
Greenock 99 Dalrymple St Greenock Renfs. PA15 1DW: 0475 24422
Grimsby 2nd Floor Bridge Ho. 225/241 Victoria St Grimsby DN31 1QL: 0472 59731

Halifax Westgate Ho. Market St Halifax HX1 1PD: 0422 56911
Harlow 12th Level Terminus Ho. The High Harlow CM20 1TX: 0279 29591
Holborn Northgate Ho. 1 Remnant St Lincoln's Inn Fields London WC2A 3JH: 01-405 8777
Hull Portcullis Ho. Queen's Gardens Hull HU1 3DS: 0482 24171

Ipswich Haven Ho. 17 Lower Brook St Ipswich IP4 1DN: 0473 212388

Kennington 206/212 Kennington Park Rd Kennington London SE11 4DD: 01-582 1024
Kingston Upon Thames Government Offices Garrison Lane Chessington KT9 2LP: 01-397 9411

Lancaster Mitre Ho. Church St Lancaster LA1 1HQ: 0524 65911
Leeds East Bank Ho. Park Place Leeds LS1 2RH: 0532 442081
Leeds West As for Leeds East
Leicester Pennine Ho. 31/33 Millstone Lane Leicester LE1 5JP: 0533 530651

VAT – A working guide for the small business

Lisburn PO Box 6 Moira Ho. 121 Hillsborough Rd Lisburn Co Antrim BT28 1LB: 08462 5171
Liverpool Custon Ho. Cunard Bldg Liverpool L3 1DX: 051-227 4343
Luton Jansel Ho. Hitchen Rd Luton LU2 7XJ: 0582 21241
Lytham St Annes Petros Ho. St Andrews Rd North Lytham St Annes FY8 2JA: 0253 721271

Maidenhead Marlow Ho. Marlow Rd Maidenhead SL6 7DU: 0628 33177
Maidstone Kent Ho. Lower Stone St Maidstone ME15 6YP: 0622 65181
Manchester Grove Ho. Skerton Rd Manchester M16 0LP: 061-872 6141
Middlesborough Church Ho. Grange Rd Middlesborough TS1 2LP: 0642 218191

Newcastle-under-Lyme Blackburn Ho. The Midway Newcastle ST5 1UT: 0782 610101/6
Newcastle-upon-Tyne Block C Government Bldgs Kenton Bar Newcastle-upon-Tyne NE1 2YU: 091-286 9811
Newport Chartist Tower Dock St Newport Gwent NPT 1XY: 0633 56271
Northampton Princess Ho. Cliftonville Rd Northampton NN1 5AE: 0604 21411
Nowich 2nd Floor Norfolk Tower Surrey St Nowich NR1 3NZ: 0603 660721
Nottingham Bowman Ho. 100/102 Talbot St Nottingham NG1 5NF: 0602 470451

Oldham Oliver Ho. Oliver St Oldham OL1 1EY: 061-652 0621
Orpington 85 The Walnuts Orpington BR6 0TN: 0689 38321
Oxford Littlegate Ho. St Ebbes St Oxford OX1 1QA: 0865 721161

Peterborough Carlton Ho. Fletton Ave Peterborough PE2 8AT: 0733 51321

Local VAT offices listing

Plymouth Pearl Assurance Ho. Royal Parade Plymouth PL1 1HQ: 0752 266641
Poole Country Gates Ho. 300 Poole Rd Poole Dorset BH12 1AQ: 0202 762366
Portsmouth Wingfield Ho. 316 Commercial Rd Portsmouth PO1 4TG: 0705 827666

Reading Premier Ho. 95/107 Southampton St Reading RG1 2QE: 0734 875345
Reigate Tower Ho. 3 Cromwell Rd Redhill RH1 1QU: 0737 68600
Romford Crown Bldgs 30 Main Rd Romford RM1 3HL: 0708 21011

Sheffield Chesham Ho. 3/7 Charter Row Sheffield S1 4HY: 0742 71261
Shrewsbury British Rail Ho. Chester St Shrewsbury SY1 1QD: 0743 61421/6
Southall Phoenix Ho. 8 The Green Southall UB2 4BZ: 01-574 8151
Southampton Roebuck Ho. 26 Bedford Place Southampton SO1 2DB: 0703/32911
Southend 9th Floor Maitland Ho. Warrior Sq Southend-on-Sea SS99 1AD: 0702 614141
Stratford 5th Floor Central Ho. 32/66 High St Stratford E15 2PX: 01-534 6611
Swansea Oldway Ho. Rutland Place Swansea SA1 3NF: 0792 42951

Taunton Brendon Ho. 35/36 High St Taunton TA1 3DR: 0823 85123
Truro Circuit Ho. St Clement St Truro TR1 1DU: 0872 74232

Washington Pennine Ho. Washington Centre Washington New Town NE37 1LU: 091 4165123
West End Wingate Ho. 93/107 Shaftesbury Ave London W1V 8HS: 01-437 9800
Westminster 67 Tufton St London SW1P 3QT: 01-222 4388
Wigan Lingate Ho. 102 Chapel Lane Wigan WN3 4BJ: 0942 44922

VAT – A working guide for the small business

Woking Bradfield Ho.
Bradfield Close York Rd Woking
GU22 7RD: 04862 69661
Wolverhampton Albany Ho. Chapel
Ash Wolverhampton WV3 0UJ: 0902
771921 and 28408/9
Worthing Teville Gate Ho. Railway
Approach Worthing BN11 1TZ:
0903 204391/8

APPENDIX II

VAT Trade Classification

Trade Code		Tax Periods Stagger Group
	PRIMARY INDUSTRIES	
	Group 01 – Agriculture, forestry and fishing	
0011	Livestock farming (including pigs and poultry)	
0012	Arable farming	
0013	Dairying	
0014	Mixed farming (no more than 50% in any of the above)	
0015	Breeding of non-food producing animals (including horses)	2
0016	Agricultural contracting	
0017	Market gardening and fruit farming	
0018	Flower and seed growing	
0020	Forestry	
0030	Fishing	
	Group 02 – Mining and quarrying	
1010	Coal mining other than opencast (heading 5030)	
1020	Stone and slate quarrying and mining	
1030	Chalk, clay, sand and gravel extraction	
1040	Petroleum and natural gas	
1090	Other mining and quarrying	
	MANUFACTURING INDUSTRIES	
	Group 03 – Food, drink and tobacco	3
2110	Grain milling	
2120	Bread and flour confectionery	
2130	Biscuits	
2140	Bacon-curing, meat and fish products	
2151	Milk and milk products (other than ice cream)	
2152	Ice cream	
2160	Sugar	

VAT – A working guide for the small business

2170	Cocoa, chocolate and sugar confectionery	
2180	Fruit and vegetable products	
2190	Animal and poultry foods	
2210	Vegetable and animal oils and fats	
2290	Food industries not elsewhere specified	3
2310	Brewing and malting	
2320	Soft drinks	
2391	Spirit distilling and compounding	
2392	British wines, cider and perry	
2400	Tobacco	

Group 04 – Coal and petroleum products
- 2610 Coke ovens and manufactured fuel
- 2620 Mineral oil refining
- 2630 Lubricating oils and greases

Group 05 – Chemicals and allied industries
- 2710 General chemicals (manufacture of chemical elements, organic and inorganic compounds (except pharmaceuticals, dyestuffs and pesticides))
- 2720 Pharmaceutical chemicals and preparations
- 2730 Toilet preparations
- 2740 Paint
- 2750 Soap and detergents
- 2760 Synthetic resins, plastics materials and synthetic rubber
- 2770 Dyestuffs and pigments
- 2780 Fertilizers
- 2790 Other chemical industries (polishes, adhesives, explosives and fireworks, pesticides, printing ink, surgical bandages, etc; photographic chemical materials)

3

Group 06 – Metal manufacture
- 3110 Iron and steel (general)
- 3120 Steel tubes
- 3130 Iron castings etc.
- 3210 Aluminium and aluminium alloys
- 3220 Copper, brass and other copper alloys
- 3230 Other base metals

Group 07 – Mechanical engineering
- 3310 Agricultural machinery (except tractors)
- 3320 Metal working machine tools
- 3330 Pumps, valves and compressors
- 3340 Industrial engines
- 3350 Textile machinery and accessories
- 3360 Construction and earth moving equipment
- 3370 Mechanical handling equipment
- 3380 Office machinery

VAT trade classification

3390	Other machinery
3410	Industrial (including process) plant and steel work
3420	Ordnance and small arms
3490	Other mechanical engineering not elsewhere specified

Group 08 – Instrument engineering

3510	Photographic and document copying equipment
3520	Watches and clocks
3530	Surgical instruments and appliances
3540	Scientific and industrial instruments and systems

Group 09 – Electrical engineering

3610	Electrical machinery
3620	Insulated wires and cables
3630	Telegraph and telephone apparatus and equipment
3640	Radio and electronic components
3651	Gramophone records and tape recordings
3659	Other broadcast receiving and sound reproducing equipment
3660	Electronic computers
3670	Radio, radar and electronic capital goods
3680	Electric appliances primarily for domestic use
3690	Other electrical goods

Group 10 – Shipbuilding, boatbuilding and marine engineering

3700	Shipbuilding, boatbuilding and marine engineering

Group 11 – Vehicles

3800	Wheeled tractor manufacturing
3811	Motor vehicle manufacturing
3812	Caravan manufacturing
3820	Motor cycle, tricycle and pedal cycle manufacturing
3830	Aerospace eqipment manufacturing and repairing
3840	Locomotives and railway track equipment
3850	Railway carriages, wagons and trams

Group 12 – Metal goods not elsewhere specified

3900	Engineers' small tools and gauges
3910	Hand tools and implements
3920	Cutlery, spoons, forks, plated tableware etc.
3930	Bolts, nuts, screws, rivets etc.
3940	Wire and wire manufactures
3950	Cans and metal boxes

3961	Jewellery manufacturing
3962	Jewellery processing
3963	Precious metals and articles of precious metal (other than jewellery)
3990	Metal industries not elsewhere specified

Group 13 – Textiles

4110	Production of man-made fibres
4120	Spinning and doubling on the cotton and flax systems
4130	Weaving of cotton, linen and man-made fibres
4140	Woollen and worsted
4150	Jute
4160	Rope, twine and net
4170	Hosiery and other knitted goods
4180	Lace
4190	Carpets
4210	Narrow fabrics (not more than 30 cm wide)
4220	Made-up textiles
4230	Textile finishing
4290	Other textile industries

Group 14 – Leather, leather goods and fur

4310	Leather (tanning and dressing) and fellmongery
4321	Handbags (including handbags of plastic and imitation leather)
4322	Travel goods (including goods of plastic and imitation leather)
4329	Other leather goods (including imitation leather)
4311	Fur processing
4339	Other fur

Group 15 – Clothing and footwear

4410	Weatherproof outerwear
4420	Men's and boy's tailored outerwear
4430	Women's and girls' tailored outerwear
4440	Overalls and men's shirts, underwear etc.
4450	Dresses, lingerie, infants' wear etc.
4460	Hats, caps and millinery
4490	Dress industries not elsewhere specified
4500	Footwear

Group 16 – Bricks, ceramics, glass, cement etc.

4610	Bricks, fireclay and refractory goods
4620	Ceramics
4630	Glass
4640	Cement
4690	Abrasives and building materials not elsewhere specified

Group 17 – Timber, furniture etc.
4710	Timber
4721	Upholstery
4722	Chair frames (other than of metal)
4729	Other furniture for home or office use
4730	Bedding etc
4740	Shop and office fitting
4750	Wooden containers and baskets
4791	Garden furniture
4799	Other miscellaneous wood and cork manufacturing

Group 18 – Paper, printing and publishing
4810	Paper and board
4820	Packaging products of paper, board and associated materials
4830	Manufactured stationery
4840	Manufactures of paper and board not elsewhere specified
4850	Printing and publishing of newspapers
4860	Printing an publishing of periodicals
4891	Publishing of books
4892	Greeting cards
4893	Prints and reproductions
4894	Bookbinding
4899	Other printing

Group 19 – Other manufacturing industries
4910	Rubber
4920	Linoleum, plastics floor-coverings, leathercloth, etc.
4930	Brushes and brooms
4940	Toys, games, children's carriages and sports equipment
4950	Miscellaneous stationers' goods
4960	Plastics products not elsewhere specified
4991	Musical instruments
4992	Imitation jewellery
4999	Other miscellaneous manufacturing industries

CONSTRUCTION
Group 20 – Construction
5001	General builders
5002	Building and civil engineering contractors
5003	Civil engineering contractors
5004	Plumbers
5005	Joiners and carpenters
5006	Painters and decorators
5007	Roofing contractors

5008	Plastering contractors	
5009	Glazing contractors	
5011	Demolition contractors	
5012	Scaffolding specialists	
5013	Reinforced concrete specialists	
5014	Heating and ventilating engineers	
5015	Electrical contractors	
5016	Asphalt and tar spraying contractors	
5017	Plant hirers	
5018	Flooring contractors	
5019	Constructional engineers	
5021	Insulating specialists	3
5022	Suspended ceiling specialists	
5023	Wall and floor tiling specialists	
5029	Specialists not elsewhere specified	
5030	Opencast coal mining	

UTILITIES

Group 21 – Gas, electricity and water

6010	Gas	
6020	Electricity	
6030	Water	

TRANSPORT AND COMMUNICATION

Group 22 – Transport and communication

7010	Railways	
7021	Omnibus and tramway services	
7022	Taxis and private-hire cars	
7030	Road haulage contracting for general hire or reward	
7040	Other road haulage	
7050	Sea transport	
7060	Port and inland water transport	
7070	Air transport	1
7080	Postal services and telecommunications	
7091	Shipping agents and forwarding agents	
7092	Travel agents	
7093	Driving instruction	
7094	Operation of car parks, toll roads and toll bridges	
7099	Other miscellaneous transport services and storage	

VAT trade classification

DISTRIBUTIVE TRADES
Group 23 – Wholesale distribution
(N.B. Wholesaling of motor vehicles (new and second-hand), including motor cycles and caravans, is allocated to heading 8941 and not to the headings within this group)

Wholesale distribution of:

8101	Fresh meat, fish, fruit and vegetables
8102	Alcoholic drink (including bottling)
8109	Other food and drink
8110	Petroleum products
8121	Chemists' sundries
8122	Clocks and watches
8123	Clothing
8124	Furs
8125	Textiles
8126	Footwear
8127	Electrical goods
8128	Radios, TV sets, tape recorders, tape recordings and gramophone records
8129	Jewellery
8131	Imitation jewellery
8132	Musical instruments
8133	Photographic goods
8134	Toys
8135	Travel and fancy goods (including shopping bags)
8136	Furniture and floor coverings
8137	China, glassware, hardware and ironmongery
8138	Paper and board products, including reading material
8139	Leasing of office furniture, vending machines, juke boxes and gaming machines
8149	Other goods

} 2

Group 24 – Retail distribution
(N.B. Retailing of motor vehicles (new and second-hand), including motor cycles and caravans, is allocated to heading 8941 and not to the headings within this group)

8201	Grocers
8202	Dairymen
8203	Butchers
8204	Fishmongers and poulterers
8205	Greengrocers and fruiterers
8206	Bread and flour confectioners
8207	Off-licences
8211	Department stores
8212	Variety and other general stores
8213	General mail order houses
8214	Confectioners, tobacconists and newsagents

} 1

8215	Footwear shops	
8216	Men's and boys' wear shops	
8217	Women's and girls' wear, household textiles and general clothing shops	
8218	Retail furriers	
8219	Domestic furniture shops, floor coverings shops, furniture and upholstery repairs	
8221	Antique dealers, second-hand furniture shops, art dealers, picture framers and dealers in stamps and coins	
8222	Radio and electrical goods shops (excluding radio and TV rental and relay shops)	
8223	Radio and TV rental shops	1
8224	Hardware, china, wallpaper and paint shops	
8225	Cycle and perambulator shops	
8226	Bookshops and stationers	
8227	Chemists and photographic shops	
8228	Opticians	
8229	Jewellery, watch and clock retailers and repairers	
8231	Leather goods, sports goods, toys and fancy goods shops	
8232	Music shops (including gramophone records)	
8233	Florists, nurserymen and garden shops	
8234	Pet and pet food shops	
8239	Other non-food shops	

Group 25 – Dealers

(N.B. Dealing in motor vehicles (new and second-hand, including motor cycles and caravans, is allocated to heading 8941 and not to the headings within this group)

8311	Coal and oil merchants (not including bulk oil distributors or petrol filling stations)	
8312	Builders' merchants	
8313	Corn, seed and agricultural merchants; dealers in livestock	2
8321	Dealing in industrial materials	
8322	Dealing in scrap and other waste materials	
8323	Dealing in industrial and agricultural machinery	
8324	Leasing industrial and office machinery	

SERVICES

Group 26 – Insurance, banking, finance and business services

8600	Insurance	
8610	Banking and bill discounting	
8612	Stockbrokers	
8622	Unit and investment trusts	3
8629	Other financial institutions	
8630	Property owning and managing etc.	

8640	Advertising and market research	
8651	Industrial and commercial valuers, auctioneers and transfer agents	
8652	Chartered or company secretaries (firms acting as)	
8653	Computer services	3
8654	Contract cleaning	
8655	Management consultants	
8656	Staff bureaux and employment agencies	
8657	Duplicating, calculating and typewriting agencies	
8659	Other business services	

Group 27 – Professional and scientific services

8710	Accountancy services	
8720	Educational services	
8730	Legal services	
8741	Hospital and consultant services	
8742	Local authority health services	
8743	General medical services	
8744	Dental services	
8749	Other medical services	
8750	Religious organisations	
8760	Research and development services	
8791	Veterinary services	3
8792	Surveying (various kinds)	
8793	Architects (private practice)	
8794	Draughtsmen (private practice)	
8795	Consultant engineers	
8796	Research chemists, analytical chemists, assayers, non-medical bacteriologists, metallurgists and geologists (private practices)	
8797	Professional and scientific representative bodies	
8798	Artists, sculptors, designers, authors, journalists (free-lance) and composers	
8799	Other professional and scientific services	

Group 28 – Miscellaneous services

8811	Cinemas	
8812	Theatres, music halls, etc; radio and television services (excluding relay services) film and recording studios, etc.	
8813	Performers and performing groups (drama, music, variety, etc.)	2
8814	Radio and television relay services	
8821	Dance halls and dancing schools	
8822	Sport	
8829	Other recreations	
8830	Betting and gaming	

8841	Hotels and other residential establishments
8842	Holiday camps, camping and holiday caravan sites
8851	Restaurants, cafes, snack bars etc. selling food for consumption on the premises only
8852	Fish and chip shops, sandwich and snack bars and other establishments selling food partly or wholly for consumption off the premises
8860	Public houses
8870	Clubs (excluding sports clubs and gaming clubs)
8880	Catering contractors
8891	Men's hairdressing and manicure
8892	Women's hairdressing and manicure
8921	Launderettes
8922	Laundries
8923	Hire of towels, linen and industrial clothing
8930	Dry cleaning, job dyeing, carpet beating etc.
8941	Distribution, repair and servicing of motor vehicles (including whoesaling, retailing and dealing in motor vehicles and caravans (new and second-hand), tyres, motor accessories and spares)
8942	Petrol filling stations
8950	Repair of boots and shoes
8991	Funeral direction, cemeteries and crematoria
8992	Photography and photographic processing
8993	Welfare and charitable services
8994	Public museums, libraries and galleries
8995	Political parties and associations
8996	Services of Commonwealth and foreign governments
8997	Trade associations and unions
8999	Other services

Group 29 – Public administration and defence

9010	National government service
9060	Local government service

APPENDIX III

Fixed retail mark-ups

VAT trade classification	Retailer type	Fixed mark-up (To be applied to the cost of positive-rated goods, including VAT)	
Band 1		16⅔%	(1/6th)
8207	Off licences		
8214	Confectioners, tobacconists and newsagents		
Band 2		20%	(1/5th)
8201	Grocers		
8202	Dairymen		
8203	Butchers		
8204	Fishmongers		
8206	Bakers		
Band 3		40%	(2/5ths)
8205	Greengrocers and fruiterers		
8222	Radio and electrical goods shops (excluding radio and TV rental and relay shops)		
8225	Cycle and perambulator shops		
8226	Bookshops and stationers		
8227	Chemists and photographic shops		
8232	Music shops (including gramophone records)		
Band 4		50%	(1/2)
All classifications from 8201 to 8239 not otherwise mentioned			
Band 5		75%	(3/4)
8229	Jewellers		

APPENDIX IV

How to check the validity of the VAT Registration Number on invoices received

VAT Registration Number shown on invoice   425 4032 85*

(1) Write the first seven numbers in a vertical column as shown below.

(2) In the second column write alongside the list the following figures – 8, 7, 6, 5, 4, 3, 2.

(3) Multiply Column 1 by Column 2.

(4) Add up the result.

(5) From this total deduct the amount of 97 as many times as is necessary to reach a negative figure.

(6) If the registration number is valid, the answer you have arrived at should be the same as the last two digits of that registration number.

Example:

Column 1		Column 2		Total
4	×	8	=	32
2	×	7	=	14
5	×	6	=	30
4	×	5	=	20
0	×	4	=	—
3	×	3	=	9
2	×	2	=	4

                                    109
                        minus   97
                                    ―――
                                     12
                        minus   97
                                    ―――
                                    -85*

This corresponds with the last two digits of the VAT registration number quoted, which is therefore valid.

Index

A
accounting period 61
appeal and review, independent 87
assets, disposal of 75

B
business, definition of 9
  records 38
  sale of a 73
  splitting, method of 82–83
businesses, partially exempt 45

C
capital expenditure 80
Companies Act, UK 24–25
credit notes 70–71
Customs and Excise, HM 7–11, 19, 21–22, 24–26, 33, 35, 38–39, 43, 47, 49, 51, 55–59, 61, 63, 65–67, 69–70, 76, 79–83, 91–93
  dealing with 85–90
  power of 87
  repayment from 13
Customs and Excise officers, powers of HM's 7

D
debt, bad 69
de-registration 27, 82, 91–95
  applying for 91
  compulsory 92
  voluntary 81
discounts 75

E
EEC (European Comminity, the) 7
  budget, UK's contribution to 7
  countries 12
  Sixth Directive 48
European Court of Justice in Luxembourg 90
exempt goods 57
  -related inputs 46
  supply 9
  supplies 11, 16–17, 26, 58
  and taxable supplies 10
exemption 17
  items of 16–17
  partial 46, 75, 77
exemptions 8
exporting businesses 8

F
Finance Act, 1972 11, 48
  Act, 1985 80, 85–86
  Act, 1987 21
Food 13
Franklin, Benjamin 7

G
gifts 49
  business 75
goods, export of 11
  importation of 11
  returned 71
  secondhand 71
  supply of 10–11
  group registration election 72

I
Inheritance Tax duties 17
'Input Rules' 77
investment income surcharge 7

K
Keith Committee, the 85

L
Land Tax, abolition of development 7
leasing transactions 76
limits, *de-minimis* 76–77

M
management charges 72
motoring expenses, VAT on 49

P
partnership, creation of 11
proforma invoice 59, 81
property, interests in 10

R

registered person 11
registration, avoiding 82
   cancellation of 50
   date of 85
   early 24
   late 85
   limit, annual 21
   limits 24
   notice of 25
   timing of 82
   voluntary 92
retail scheme 26
returns, late 86
rule, *de-minimus* 45–46
   50 per cent 32

S

Scheme A 30
   B 32
   B1 32
   B2 32
   C 32–33
   D 33
   E 34
   F 34
   G 33
   H 35
   J 35
   Annual Accounting 36
   of Cash Accounting 35
Schemes, A,B,C,D,E,F,G,H,J 29
   retail 29–39
self-billing system 58–59
service industries, the 81
   supply of 11
services, free supply of 48
standard-rated supplies 26
stock account 43
supply, date of 56
   place of 51–52
   time of 51
   value of 52
surcharge liability 63
   liability notice 86

T

tax, capital transfer 7
   cascade 41
   current rate of 10
   input 10–11, 21–22, 24, 26, 41–46, 49, 51–52, 62, 65, 73, 75–77, 79, 82, 86, 89, 93
   invoice 70
   invoice, modified 58
   invoice, proper 44
   liability for arrears of 19
   output 10, 21, 26, 32–34, 43, 47–53, 59, 61–62, 82, 86, 93
   point 42–43, 51, 55–56
   positive rate of 11, 13, 33, 38
   pre-registration input 43
   purchase 7
   rate of 8
   relief, input 45
   selection employment 7
   standard rate of 32, 45
   zero rate of 11, 38, 51
   zero-rated 45, 75, 79, 80–81
Tax, Corporation 72
   Evasion 85
taxable person 11
   supplies 11, 19, 47
taxation, direct 7
Taxpayers Charter, the 87
trade classification 19
traders, seasonal 9
turnover, taxable 8, 19, 21–22

V

Value Added Tax Act (VATA), 1973 8
VAT accounting records 25
   Certificate of Registration 25
   default notice 63
   default surcharges 62
   exempt supplies 44
   error 89
   Freeport 52
   general accounting for 38
   group registration 76
   input 38
   inspections 88
   intake, UK 46
   invoice 22, 26, 55–59

legislation governing 8
man, visit from 88
mechanics of 13
output 34, 38
planning 79–83, 93–95
quarter, the selected 21
reclaiming 21
records 22, 38, 55
registration 8, 10–11, 19–27, 69, 91–92
registration number 22, 25, 73
regulations 9, 83
relief for bad debts 69–70
return 25, 33, 42–43, 61–67, 89, 93
rules, current 8
standard rate of 47
submissions, penalties for late 62
system, workings of 8
trading threshold 91
tribunal 92
types of 13–17
voluntary registration 21–22, 25
zero rate of 47

Z
zero-rated categories 13–15
   -rated goods 8, 32, 57
   -rated supply 11, 19, 21–22, 26, 58
   rating 12, 16–17

A DAILY TELEGRAPH BUSINESS ENTERPRISE BOOK

How to Set Up and Run Conferences and Meetings

Will it be Benidorm, Brighton or just the back office?

Don't panic – for the first time there is a book designed to take you through each stage of arranging your conference or meeting.

Packed full of useful tips to ensure that, however large or small, the operation is a success.

This invaluable handbook details:

- Types of conference and their themes
- Budgeting – how to minimise expenditure
- Drawing up the agenda
- The importance of a suitable venue
- Presentation equipment – the most suitable audio and video techniques
- Holding the audience's attention
- Making the arrangements
- Conference catering
- Planning conferences abroad
- Has it been a success? – including a range of case studies

How to Set Up and Run Conferences and Meetings simplifies the whole procedure by outlining the numerous options. It includes a timetable and detailed checklist to help you avoid the possible pitfalls and ensure a successful, productive conference or meeting.

Written by experts, this practical guide is an essential tool for every office. For anyone – from the Managing Director to the secretary – who is charged with this difficult task.

£6.95 paperback, £11.95 hardback net in UK

A DAILY TELEGRAPH BUSINESS ENTERPRISE BOOK

Motivating through Incentives

How do you decide whether or not your company should be using incentives internally to motivate its personnel, or externally to stimulate suppliers', dealers' or agents' interest.

Have you considered:

- What types of incentives are available?
- Which of these best meets the aims of your company?
- Who should be offered incentives and for what reason?
- What is it going to cost and what are the tax implications for both your company and the individuals involved?

Motivating through Incentives answers these and the many other questions which arise about the growing use of 'gifts in kind'. It illustrates possible applications through a selection of appropriate Case Studies and shows how to assess your company's incentive programme for tax purposes.

In today's fast-moving business environment a competitive spirit in sales, whatever the size of your organisation, is the lifeblood of any company and *Motivating through Incentives* fulfills a vital role in helping you to maximise the potential available to you. This book should be on the bookshelf – if not in the briefcase – of every dynamic, forward-looking business person.

The author, Ken Gazzard, has had over 20 years experience with one of the largest motivational incentive firms in the USA. He pioneered the use of incentives by both British and European companies and is a well-known expert in this field.

Publication date: August 1987
£6.95 paperback net in UK

A DAILY TELEGRAPH BUSINESS ENTERPRISE HANDBOOK

PCs at Work

Are you thinking of buying a microcomputer for your business? Do you want to know more about what microcomputers can do for you? Do you think you need a computer to make your job easier or more interesting but do not know how to justify the cost? This *Daily Telegraph Business Handbook* tells you everything you need to know, simply and clearly, without jargon or technicalities. The book is packed with advice from users who have had experience of buying and living with systems – advice that helps you make the best decisions and avoid the pitfalls.

PCs at Work answers all your questions:

- Does a microcomputer offer a solution to my most pressing business problems?
- Will it save me money?
- Will it make my business easier to run?
- How can I convince my colleagues that it is worth the expense?
- How do I choose the best package?
- What do the complicated technical phrases mean in everyday practice?
- What problems should I expect and how do I avoid the pitfalls?
- Do I need to spend time reading computer magazines?

This indispensable book takes you step-by-step through all the decisions you will need to take. It contains invaluable forms to assist you in your decision-making and tells you exactly what to expect from the software you will want to use – for accounting, word processing, filing. The full glossary will help you out if you are ever at a loss.

If you are thinking about buying a microcomputer for your business, buy this book first. It will save you time, money and effort.

Publication date: September 1987
£5.95 paperback net in UK

CHECKLIST

Your VAT number: _____

Local H.M. Customs and _____
Excise address: _____
_____

Telephone No: _____
Name of local Inspector: _____
Telephone No: _____
Extension: _____

Selected retail scheme: _____

Stagger group: _____

CHECKLIST

Turnover for first year   _____

Turnover for second year   _____

VAT amount payable   _____

    1st quarter   _____

    2nd quarter   _____

    3rd quarter   _____

    4th quarter   _____

Cheque sent   _____

    1st quarter   _____

    2nd quarter   _____

    3rd quarter   _____

    4th quarter   _____